"THE CONSPIRACY THEORY FRAUD"

VOLUME ONE
"THE FRAUD OF THE FRAUD"

Prepared and Translated by Jose M. Paulino

-Written in plain language-

The Sacred Movement

Copyright © 2008
"THE FRAUD OF THE FRAUD" (VOLUME 1)

Where Conspiracy Facts Meet Conspiracy Theories

Author: Jose M. Paulino

Editor: Natalia Paulino

Research funded by OneSource Financial.

Printed in the U.S.A.

ISBN: 1440471886

EAN-13: 9781440471889

COVER DESIGN BY:
Jose M. Paulino

Contact Info:
Thefraud12@gmail.com

-For more information, or to purchase additional copies of this written documentary (BOOK), go to the following link:
http://www.factsmovement.com/

"THE FRAUD OF THE FRAUD"

Fasten your seat belts true believers, because the road that leads to facts is a bumpy one...............

A WRITTEN DOCUMENTARY

Volume One.....................

Table of Contents

THIS BOOK IS <u>DEDICATED</u> TO ALL THAT SEEK PEACE, AND IT IS <u>GIVEN</u> TO THOSE WHO SEEK RIGHT KNOWLEDGE.

PREFACE

This book is the first part of a series of written documentaries aimed at educating, informing, and empowering the people to take back what has been taken from them through fraud. This volume was first published on October 20, 2008 together with volume two in a 286 page 8"x10" cover; ISBN 1438-261918. It is the purpose of these documentaries to gather the most valuable information of all types. The goal is to put the information in such a form, that it may be of service to those who seek right knowledge. This documentary will attempt to present material that one may not only find interesting, but will also find worth exploring beyond the confines of this book.

PRE- INTRODUCTION

I do not expect anyone to believe the information found within the confines of this book, nor will I claim that there are no errors in this book—whether grammatical, historical, or mathematical. Human error will occur even with inspired work. This book is only intended to inform you of doctrines, methods, and information that you may not be aware of. It is the responsibility of those who seek truth and knowledge to do their very own due diligence on any subject or information that intrigues them.

Having an open mind does not mean believing or accepting things that are not proven to be true. Having an open mind means accepting information on its face, as oppose to rejecting it simply because you believe or have been taught something to the contrary. Remember, if something is true, it does not matter whether you believe it or not. As a great teacher once said "Truth is truth." One who is informed is one who has learned both or all sides of a story. Only then can a person make an informed decision. If you only have one side of a story and reject the other side without combing through it, you are ill-informed. This is why religious people are ill-informed. They have chosen their religion without studying all others. The racists are ill-informed because they have chosen their race to be the best without understanding the struggles or accomplishments of other races. I can go on. However, those two important topics will suffice for this pre-introduction. Therefore, as you read through these pages, keep in mind that I am not trying to make you believe anything, nor convince you of anything. I am merely informing you of something that is different from what you have been taught. If you do not explore both sides of a story, you will remain ill-informed.

I will try my best to document all relevant facts quoted in this book. Thanks to the internet, your trips to the library will be limited. However, it will still be up to you, the individual, to check it out for yourself. Belief is ignorance. To know is knowledge. For that reason, this book is meant to educate and inform people who I consider friends and family. The intention of this book is not meant to offend anyone or make light of anyone's ideas and beliefs. It is best suited to inform those who have no idea they are constantly being lied to and led astray. It is also suited for those who are confined to a single ideology, and with it believe that they have a monopoly on truth.

> *For, since the one who writes recognizes, by the very fact that he takes the trouble to write, the freedom of his readers, and since the one who reads, by the mere fact of his opening the book, recognizes the freedom of the writer, the work of art, from whichever side you approach it, is an act of confidence in the freedom of man.*

-Jean-Paul Sartre (June 21, 1905 – April 15, 1980)

INTRODUCTION

I understand the dangers of writing this type of documentary because I am going up against the human beast. Within the last 25 to 50 years, there have been many books written and lectures given concerning our problem. Today, many people around the world are waking up to what I refer to as, "The fraud of the fraud." At every level of our society, there is fraud. The criminal elite, who pull the strings that control our lives, only deal in fraud. Most people (for the most part) are ignorant to almost anything that is important or essential to their basic freedoms. Without any factual basis whatsoever, many people accept certain things as being true. This is pure ignorance. An example of this ignorance occurs when a person attempts to defend their beliefs against verified facts. If ignorance could be compared to a disease, it would (in all probability) be more than 10 times deadlier than the Ebola and Aids Viruses combined. Ignorance has killed, enslaved, and starved more people on the planet than any dictator or armed forces. But who benefits from the ignorance of the masses?

The average American believes they are in a free country. Yet, if you ask them to explain how the government of a free country works, you will get a blank "deer in the headlights" look. The average American can't name the three branches of government, much less explain their function. In view of the fact that we do not know how a free country is supposed to operate, the criminal elite can easily introduce the following: Fascism, communism, socialism, and even a clear dictatorship. This is what has happened in the United States. Out of a population of nearly 300 million people, how many have knowledge that the President of the United States does not have the authority to declare war? Only Congress can declare war. Many good people, who are against the war in Iraq, say that the war is "Unethical." However, you rarely hear anyone refer to the war as "Illegal." If the war is illegal, then it means someone should go to the iron house (jail).

Unfortunately, our level of ignorance is much deeper than not knowing the functions of government. Our ignorance

xi

takes us directly into the master/slave relationship. In addition, because we have been misled into believing that a slave is only a person who is in chains, we have unknowingly become willing participants of our own enslavement. This is a very sophisticated form of slavery. The old "ball and chains" type of slavery is primitive. The criminal elite who run this planet learned that the people will always rebel against that type of slavery. In the primitive form of slavery, a slave knew where he stood. He knew he was a slave. Today, we willingly participate because we believe we are free. This means we will never rebel. Why would anyone rebel if they believe they are free? This is what the movie "Matrix" was about. If you believe this is far fetched, test the real matrix. You will quickly find that what I am revealing is true and real.

Do something simple. Write a letter to the Social Security Administration Office of Public Inquiries. Thank them for their services and inform them that you no longer wish to participate in their program. Put them on notice of your status as a free person. Remind them that no one, especially the government, can force you to do business (contract). No person(s), especially the government, can force you to accept welfare, charity, or any type of benefit. If I offer you a $100, you have the right to not accept it. Do you see how simple it is? How can they force you to accept the $100????

The Social Security Act (Act of August 14, 1935) [H. R. 7260]

PREAMBLE

An act to provide for the general welfare by establishing a system of Federal old-age benefits, and by enabling the several States to make more adequate provision for aged persons, blind persons, dependent and crippled children, maternal and child welfare, public health, and the administration of their unemployment compensation laws; to establish a Social Security Board; to raise revenue; and for other purposes.

If you write a letter, or speak to any government agency (which are supposed to be set up for your benefit) and ask them to buzz off, you will find that what I am saying is true. You will realize that you are forced to participate in their programs against your will. If that sounds like a free society to you, then welcome to "The fraud of the fraud."

Write to the Social Security Office of Public Inquiries and ask for instructions on how to cancel your membership to the Social Security program.

Social Security Administration
Office of Public Inquiries
Windsor Park Building
6401 Security Blvd
Baltimore, MD 21235

The criminal elite are readers of space and time. Whenever they sense that a jig is up, be it slavery, racism, sexism, or whatever, they take over the mess they created in the first place and appoint their minions as the saviors. This enables them to direct their created mess to wherever it suits their needs. The first thing they do is blame the mess (they purposely created) on an enemy. Then they offer the people the solution of how to defeat that enemy. The solution always involves giving up money, property or civil liberties.

They pass laws that appear benevolent on the surface. However, most laws are designed to extract revenue from the slave population. And yet, by no means is money the underlying goal of the criminal elite. Their goal is total control and domination of humanity. It does not matter if you are poor, rich, black, white, Jew, Arab, Hindu, tall, skinny, fat, short, Christian, Buddhist, etc... THEY OWN YOU!!! You may not accept that fact. However, what you feel or believe is irrelevant to reality. After you read some of the facts and ideas within these writings, you will begin to transform back into a responsible being. We are all responsible for the lack of peace on this planet.

Within these writings, you may also recognize the work of many teachers who have helped in this struggle against the criminal elite. You may not agree with some of their teachings. You may believe that they are "this" or "they are that." You may even believe that they are simply crazy. However, truth is truth and it does not matter who spews it. This written documentary is the great culmination of eighteen years experience and research. I would like to acknowledge the generous individuals who have helped bring it to fruition. With that said, you might be familiar with the teachings of the following:

Dr. Malachi Z. York
Elijah Muhammad **(Peace be upon him)**
David Icke
Alex Jones
Anthony J. Hilder
Myron Fagan **(Peace be upon him)**
Jordan Maxwell
Jim Tucker
Richard Cornforth
Aaron Russo **(peace be upon him)**
Malcolm X **(Peace be upon him)**
Michael Tsarion
Dr. Phil Valentine
Jim Maars
Kwame Ture **(Peace be upon him)**
Irwin Schiff
Marc Stevens
Taj Tariq Bey

<u>VOLUME ONE</u>

"The Conspiracy Theory Fraud"

"It is a capital mistake to theorize before one has data. Insensibly one begins to twist facts to suit theories, instead of theories to suit facts."
Sherlock Holmes in "A Scandal in Bohemia" (1891)

1

THE CONSPIRACY FRAUD

Can human beings make a serious effort to distinguish between the idiom of an unfounded theory and the discovery of verifiable information and facts? People usually decline to accept the most convincing proof of a conspiracy for fear of admitting to themselves they have been lied to by trusted officials. It is currently common practice, in the United States of America and all over the planet, to simply dismiss any piece of information that can puncture a hole in any widely accepted explanation of a disturbing event. Far too often, especially when a serious crime may have taken place, the infamous "conspiracy theory" tag is immediately attached to any new discovery about the event. Key information related to important topics such as 9/11, JFK Assassination, the one world government, or the creation of aids is almost always ignored as part of a baseless conspiracy theory. This takes place even before any of its evidence is ever presented, discussed, or evaluated.

There is a famous line used by religious people which states, "The devil's greatest trick was to make people believe that he did not exist." However, many of those same religious people will dispute and refute any notion that there exist a small band of nefarious human beings controlling the masses. Everyone is afraid of the word "conspiracy." If you feel something isn't right or something does not add up, you better keep it to yourself. Otherwise, you may be called a "conspiracy theorist."

According to Webster's New Collegiate Dictionary, p. 243 (8th ed. 1976), to *conspire* means, *"To join in a secret agreement to do an unlawful or wrongful act or to use such means to accomplish a lawful end."* If the Bush administration planned to attack Iraq shortly after taking office and didn't tell the American people, does that fit the definition of conspiring? As you read this documentary, you will find that those who you have entrusted to run government and protect your liberties fit the very definition of "to conspire." A very important strategy used to discredit anyone who attempts to expose conspirators is to paint the exposers as "paranoid crazies."

CONSPIRACISM

Conspiracism is a term usually referred to as a broad world view that puts conspiracy theories in the unfolding history of the planet. The term Conspiracism was popularized by academic Frank P. Mintz in the 1980s. In a book entitled *"The Liberty Lobby and the American Right: Race, Conspiracy, and Culture;* Greenwood Press (March 27, 1985), Mr. Mintz states the following:

> *"Conspiracism serves the needs of diverse political and social groups in America and elsewhere. It identifies elites, blames them for economic and social catastrophes, and assumes that things will be better once popular action can remove them from positions of power. As such, conspiracy theories do not typify a particular epoch or ideology". p.1*

This doctrine is prominent among those who have been charged with keeping you asleep. In actuality, diverse political and social groups are misled into believing they can identify the "Unknowns." As an example, in the United States people believe the Republicans and Democrats have different agendas. People believe one administration is totally removed from previous administrations. However, nothing could be further from the truth. The people do not recognize who the elites really are. The average person has no idea about groups such as the Bilderbergs, the Trilateral Commission, and the Council on Foreign Relations (just to name a few). The History Channel aired a program called "Secret Societies," in where a member of the Council on Foreign Relations named Daniel Pipes attempts to downplay the existence of any conspiracies throughout history. But why would Pipes denounce his masters? He wouldn't! Let us see who and what this guy is connected to.

1. He served as an advisor to Rudolph Giuliani's 2008 presidential campaign.

2. In 2003, baby Bush nominated Pipes for the board of the United States Institute of Peace. However, after a controversy, including a filibuster by Democratic senators, Pipes obtained the position by recess appointment.

3. Pipes set up an organization called Campus Watch. This group was set up to basically be a spy network of students. The students would report anything out of the norm that was taught by Professors.

A professor and scholar from Duke University, Miriam Cooke, criticized Campus Watch by stating:

> *"Campus Watch is the Trojan horse whose warriors are already changing the rules of the game not only in Middle East studies but also in the US University as a whole. They threaten to undermine the very foundations of American education."*

Two political science scholars, John Mearsheimer and Stephen Walt, wrote a paper which was later turned into a book entitled "*The Israel Lobby and U.S. Foreign Policy,*" in which they wrote;

> *"The Lobby also monitors what professors write and teach. In September 2002, for example, Martin Kramer and Daniel Pipes, two passionately pro-Israel neoconservatives, established a website (Campus Watch) that posted dossiers on suspect academics ... This transparent attempt to blacklist and intimidate scholars prompted a harsh reaction and Pipes and Kramer later removed the dossiers."*

Refer to: http://www.arabworldbooks.com/Articles/article54.htm

Campus Watch is typical of the spy programs that have been implemented in America, whereby, everyone is spying on everyone and reporting them just like they did in Nazi-Germany. Their attempt is to make sure professors do not teach the kids how to think for themselves. Under Campus Watch, a professor could be ousted if that professor taught or spoke against the government. This is clearly not freedom! A professor's views and ideas—derived from scholarly work—must be his or her own, freely chosen. A professor or any textbook can only serve as a guide to point a student toward knowledge. By the same token, this documentary is my view, freely chosen.

Although I am greatly indebted to all those wonderful teachers mentioned in the introduction, the knowledge within this documentary rests on no other authority, either past or present. In its finality, it will stand or it will fall on its own merits. It will succeed in relation to whether it squares with the reader's own experience, and with the facts as the reader sees them. This is why it is important to view all sides of a conflict or argument before you conclude which to support. It is the same as being familiar with only two colors—let us say, blue and red. You may believe red is your favorite color. However, this is due to the fact that you have not been taught the existence of other colors. Once you can step outside of what you have been taught is the norm, you will be better equipped to make an informed decision.

In today's sophisticated world (using the color example), if you ask about other colors, they will say you are abnormal. This is the concept that makes us police each other. The concept teaches that if you question those who are in power, you must have psychological issues. The people who have an opinion which differs from that of the so-called intellectuals are viewed as abnormal or insane. If you do not agree with the conclusion of a government investigation, you are called a conspiracy theorist. If your information is different from what those in government are saying, then you have to be speaking in theory and not in fact.

Let us take the tragic events of 9/11 as an example. What is the difference between a conspiracy theory and the unproven details of what you were told happened? We were told that eighteen or nineteen Arabs with simple box cutters hi-jacked four American airliners. As the story goes, these eighteen or so Arabs plotted from a cave somewhere. Could you imagine trying to pull something like this off with eighteen of your buddies? How smart would you and your buddies have to be? How smart were the hi-jackers? According to reports, they had average jobs and were of average intelligence! How could they get passed the most sophisticated country in the world? That story, in and of itself, is a conspiracy theory. Nineteen dumb-asses conspired and pulled off a miracle! If it wasn't for the tragedy of all the people who lost their lives that day, it would be comical. What evidence was proffered to solidify such nonsense? What if this string of events was given to you by a so-called conspiracy theorist? Would you question the story? When it was revealed that some of these so-called hi-jackers were still alive, would you have called the conspiracy theorist a liar? Why aren't the people who fed you that story called liars? Why do they get a pass? Why do you believe that they have your best interest at heart, and why do you believe that they could never do such things? Why do we "the people" continue to trust them?

How many lies and inconsistencies do we have to un-cover before we understand, it is not a conspiracy theory? It is just a plain old conspiracy! But wait.... Let me correct myself. We can no longer say it is a conspiracy because they have so much control over our minds that they do things out in the open.

They do not even try to hide things anymore. It is amazing how they will do something out in the open, in plain view, and when someone like me informs you about what they, themselves, have admitted, I am still tagged as a crazy conspiracy theorist. That is absolutely mind boggling. It reminds me of the old Bugs Bunny cartoons, where Bugs Bunny continually denies, denies, denies, and then sneaks an admission after the denials. The sudden admission causes Bugs Bunny's adversary to also change up and reverse by telling bugs bunny that he did not do it.

In a speech that baby Bush gave at the United Nations, shortly after the 9/11 Terror Attacks, he stated; "Never let us tolerate outrageous conspiracy theories concerning the attacks of September the eleventh." (Meaning, don't question the official story)

I agree with baby Bush 100% on that issue. Therefore, I do not tolerate that suicide hi-jackers smashed airplanes into skyscrapers and survived the crash. This is the world we live in. George W. Bush can tell you not to believe anything other than what the government has told you happened (even if it's ridiculous). Meanwhile, he lobbied to block a real investigation of the attacks.

The New York Times

Stonewalled by the C.I.A.
By THOMAS H. KEAN and LEE H. HAMILTON
Published: January 2, 2008

(In part)

"The commission's mandate was sweeping and it explicitly included the intelligence agencies. But the recent revelations that the C.I.A. destroyed videotaped interrogations of Qaeda operatives leads us to conclude that the agency failed to respond to our lawful requests for information about the 9/11 plot. Those who knew about those videotapes — and did not tell us about them — obstructed our investigation.

There could have been absolutely no doubt in the mind of anyone at the C.I.A. — or the White House — of the commission's interest in any and all information related to Qaeda detainees involved in the 9/11 plot. Yet no one in the administration ever told the commission of the existence of videotapes of detainee interrogations."

CNN.com.

FBI: Early probe results show 18 hijackers took part

September 13, 2001 Posted: 10:33 PM EDT (0233 GMT)

FBI Director Robert Mueller

WASHINGTON (CNN) -- With U.S. authorities saying they believe they have identified most of the hijackers responsible for Tuesday's terrorist attacks, investigators cast an international net for accomplices, believed to be "a significant number."

FBI Director Robert Mueller said a preliminary investigation indicated 18 hijackers were on the four planes -- five on each of the two planes that crashed into the World Trade Center, and four each on the planes that crashed into the Pentagon and in Pennsylvania.

The widening investigation stretched from the Canadian border to Florida, from Pennsylvania into Europe, as U.S. investigators enlisted the help of the international law enforcement community.

U.S. Attorney General John Ashcroft said a team of 4,000 special agents at the FBI, joined by 3,000 support personnel, are working on the largest investigation in U.S. history. Thousands perished when two hijacked commercial jets slammed into the World Trade Center's twin towers Tuesday morning, causing the 110-story towers to collapse in a terrifying cascade of cement, metal, glass and human bodies. A third jet slammed into the Pentagon, and a fourth crashed in rural Pennsylvania.
Among the developments:
-- Ashcroft said the pilots who hijacked the four planes were trained in the United States and had ground support.
-- U.S. Secretary of State Colin Powell named suspected terrorist mastermind Osama bin Laden as one of the primary suspects in the hijackings and crashes.
-- Investigators leading the probe of the Pennsylvania jetliner crash said they found debris six miles away from the crash site.

CORRECTION

We would like to correct a report that appeared on CNN. Based on information from multiple law enforcement sources, CNN reported that Adnan Bukhari and Ameer Bukhari of Vero Beach Florida, were suspected to be two of the pilots who crashed planes into the World Trade Center. CNN later learned that Adnan Bukhari is still in Florida, where he was questioned by the FBI. We are sorry for the misinformation. A federal law enforcement source now tells CNN that Bukhari passed an FBI polygraph and is not considered a suspect. Through his attorney, Bukhari says that he is helping authorities. Ameer Bukhari died in a small plane crash last year.

This article can be found in its totality at
http://archives.cnn.com/2001/US/09/13/investigation.terrorism/index.html as of 3/26/08

The text box on the right only appeared on CNN.com. Why is it that the masses do not know some of these guys were found alive and well? Why didn't this make major news? Why isn't it mentioned in the 911 Commission? Why haven't they come out and told the people that the identities of the hijackers are in doubt? The fact that some of the hi-jackers were still alive was reported in more detail in foreign media outlets. However, in the United States, it was mostly silent. We were busy waiving our flags and drinking the Kool-Aid that was pouring out of Washington.

The FBI press release of September 27, 2001, containing names, photographs, aliases and other information is seriously flawed. They have used these people's names and made claims based on the fact they were pilots—along with other supposedly incriminating evidence. And yet, they were not even remotely involved in the attacks. Places of birth, birthdates, and other personal details were displayed on news throughout the world. The following is the FBI's statement in its press release (which can still be read in it's entirety at the following website: http://www.fbi.gov/pressrel/pressrel01/092701hjpic.htm), they actually stated:

> *"It should be noted that attempts to confirm the true identities of these individuals are still under way. The FBI asks anyone who has ever seen or has information about these individuals to immediately contact the nearest FBI office or the toll free hotline number."*

Even 'til this day, the FBI continues to list these men as hijackers killed during the terror attack. This is absurd! If this is the quality of evidence they can present to the public, no wonder we cannot see the rest of it. They hide behind the infamous "Matter of national security" speech. That is what they drum up every time the people sense they are hiding something. It is the "national security" theme that still does not allow us to see the surveillance videos of the alleged American Airlines plane that hit the Pentagon. The same nonsense, 'til this day, does not allow us to see the surveillance tapes that were almost immediately confiscated from many local businesses shortly after the 1995 Oklahoma Bombing fiasco. I am not suggesting that nothing qualifies as a matter for national security. I am saying that if the before mentioned tapes only show what the government has claimed happened, how would the national security be affected? For instance, if an American airliner hit the Pentagon, why can't we see it? We saw the planes hit the towers and national security stood still. How could a foreign enemy gain an advantage by viewing the complete footage of the attack on the Pentagon?

Furthermore, Timothy McVeigh is dead. The official story says he was alone in the Ryder Truck. How can national security be disrupted if they show McVeigh in and around the truck before the blast? What would change? Nothing would change. Unless of course, they are lying about what has really taken place.

The following BBC article can be found at: http://news.bbc.co.uk/1/hi/world/middle_east/1559151.stm as of 4/15/08. It was published a week and a half after the attacks took place.

Sunday, 23 September, 2001, 12:30 GMT 13:30 UK

Hijack 'suspects' alive and well

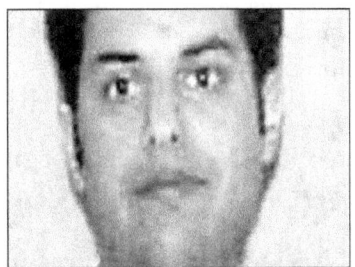

A man called Waleed Al Shehri says he left the US a year ago

Another of the men named by the FBI as a hijacker in the suicide attacks on Washington and New York has turned up alive and well.

The identities of four of the 19 suspects accused of having carried out the attacks are now in doubt.

Saudi Arabian pilot Waleed Al Shehri was one of five men that the FBI said had deliberately crashed American Airlines flight 11 into the World Trade Centre on 11 September.

His photograph was released, and has since appeared in newspapers and on television around the world.

Now he is protesting his innocence from Casablanca, Morocco.

He told journalists there that he had nothing to do with the attacks on New York and Washington, and had been in Morocco when they happened. He has contacted both the Saudi and American authorities, according to Saudi press reports.

He acknowledges that he attended flight training school at Daytona Beach in the United States, and is indeed the same Waleed Al Shehri to whom the FBI has been referring.

But, he says, he left the United States in September last year, became a pilot with Saudi Arabian airlines and is currently on a further training course in Morocco.

Hijacking suspects

Flight 175: Marwan Al-Shehhi, Fayez Ahmed, Mohald Alshehri, Hamza Alghamdi and Ahmed Alghamdi

Flight 11: Waleed M Alshehri, Wail Alshehri, Mohamed Atta, Abdulaziz Alomari and Satam Al Suqami

Flight 77: Khalid Al-Midhar, Majed Moqed, Nawaq Alhamzi, Salem Alhamzi and Hani Hanjour

Flight 93: Ahmed Alhaznawi, Ahmed Alnami, Ziad Jarrahi and Saeed Alghamdi

Mistaken identity

Abdulaziz Al Omari, another of the Flight 11 hijack suspects, has also been quoted in Arab news reports.

He says he is an engineer with Saudi Telecoms, and that he lost his passport while studying in Denver.

Another man with exactly the same name surfaced on the pages of the English-language Arab News.

The second Abdulaziz Al Omari is a pilot for Saudi Arabian Airlines, the report says.

Abdelaziz Al Omari 'lost his passport in Denver'

Meanwhile, Asharq Al Awsat newspaper, a London-based Arabic daily, says it has interviewed Saeed Alghamdi.

He was listed by the FBI as a hijacker in the United flight that crashed in Pennsylvania.

And there are suggestions that another suspect, Khalid Al Midhar, may also be alive.

FBI Director Robert Mueller acknowledged on Thursday that the identity of several of the suicide hijackers is in doubt.

Khalid Al-Midhar may also be alive

(The topic of 9/11 and state sponsored terror will be covered in Volume Two "The War on Terror Fraud." The point being made here is that many believe whatever the press spews onto the mainstream media must be true. However, if someone presents something logical to indicate that something is not right, they are automatically labeled a conspiracy nut. With that type of thinking by the public, if there is a conspiracy, how easy would the conspirators have it?)

If we question everything and everyone, we can over-come. Stop blindly believing things. Rely only on facts and sound, right reasoning, also referred to as common sense. If something does not make sense, do not believe it. It does not make it a falsehood, but why does it warrant your belief? This is how we fell into trouble in the first place. We are taught to believe that it is okay to blindly accept things. They know that once they can get you to believe in something, you will act according to what it is you believe. Then, the acting that stems from belief becomes habit. It becomes a habit to the point where, you will do things without knowing why you do them. With that in your pocket, let us look at the conspiracy fraud.

A conspiracy theory is mostly based on belief. The word "theory" is akin to the word belief. If you have a theory, you do not have facts. If you have facts, they cannot be called theories. For example, it is not a theory that you are reading this book. It would also be incorrect to say, "I believe that I am reading this book." It is a fact that you are reading this book. The point I am making is that the very term "conspiracy theory" helps cast a doubt before any information is ever examined. It is a psycho-logical trick.

Most people hear the words "conspiracy theory" and it automatically triggers something that tells them, "This is not based on facts." However, so-called conspiracy theories jump into action when people decide to use their brain. They present evidence or facts that are in plain site to disprove or at least raise legitimate questions. These questions help explain the lies fed to the people (usually without any evidence) by the government or their three letter agencies (CIA, FBI, NSA, etc.). This is how the crazy conspiracy nut is born. However, there is really nothing crazy about it. On the contrary, what is really crazy would be to believe what the government tells the media to tell you. What I find insane about this whole mess is the fact that, if you ask the average person whether they believe the government lies, they will undoubtedly say, "Yes." Can we see how insane this is? It is dangerous to judge the world according to what the mainstream media feeds the public. However, throughout this documentary I will quote the mainstream media, not because they mean well, but rather to show you that they do admit a great many things.

Nevertheless, you cannot see them unless you can connect the dots. I am not claiming that the average news reporter is involved in a conspiracy. Most reporters want to do a good job and honestly report the news. On the other hand, they have their bosses influencing them to kill certain stories. The majority of the time they will reassign the reporter to work on a story that is unimportant. In addition, most reporters have been raised reading the same contorted news. By the time they get their jobs, their sense of reality is already unrealistic. They cannot fathom the wickedness of government officials or corporate heads.

Media people quickly learn how to spin stories and massage the public's ignorance. It is not always what they say, but rather, it is what they do not say. They will inundate you with O.J. Simpson, Brittany Spears, Paris Hilton, and any other unimportant person found within the public eye. What do any of these people have to do with your life? This is done purposely to keep you asleep at the wheel. They do not want an informed public. An informed person is an intelligent person. They cannot afford to have a population of people who can think for themselves. For this reason they must control the news. In today's world there is no dividing line between the government and any of the major news outlets. For example, the military analysts that were chosen by the Pentagon to cover the War on Terror were also personally involved in helping several companies acquire no-bid military contracts. This is criminal on its face! They calmly report it on the news and no one is arrested. There is no attempt to bring these criminals to justice. The U.S. Department of Justice is a joke. But hey, I think little Lindsey Lohan was just arrested for cocaine possession, details at 6:00 o'clock...

The New York Times

MESSAGE MACHINE

Behind TV Analysts, Pentagon's Hidden Hand

By DAVID BARSTOW
Published: April 20, 2008

A PENTAGON CAMPAIGN Retired officers have been used to shape terrorism coverage from inside the TV and radio networks.

In the summer of 2005, the Bush administration confronted a fresh wave of criticism over Guantánamo Bay. The detention center had just been branded "the gulag of our times" by Amnesty International, there were new allegations of abuse from United Nations human rights experts and calls were mounting for its closure.

The administration's communications experts responded swiftly. Early one Friday morning, they put a group of retired military officers on one of the jets normally used by Vice President Dick Cheney and flew them to Cuba for a carefully orchestrated tour of Guantánamo.

To the public, these men are members of a familiar fraternity, presented tens of thousands of times on television and radio as "military analysts" whose long service has equipped them to give authoritative and unfettered judgments about the most pressing issues of the post-Sept. 11 world.

Hidden behind that appearance of objectivity, though, is a Pentagon information apparatus that has used those analysts in a campaign to generate favorable news coverage of the administration's wartime performance, an examination by The New York Times has found.

The effort, which began with the buildup to the Iraq war and continues to this day, has sought to exploit ideological and military allegiances, and also a powerful financial dynamic: Most of the analysts have ties _to military contractors vested in the very war policies they are asked to assess on air._

Those business relationships are hardly ever disclosed to the viewers, and sometimes not even to the networks themselves. But collectively, the men on the plane and several dozen other military analysts represent more than 150 military contractors either as lobbyists, senior executives, board members or consultants. The companies include defense heavyweights, but also scores of smaller companies, all part of a vast assemblage of contractors scrambling for hundreds of billions in military business generated by the administration's war on terror. It is a furious competition, one in which inside information and easy access to senior officials are highly prized.

Records and interviews show how the Bush administration has used its control over access and information in an effort to transform the analysts into a kind of media Trojan horse — an instrument intended to shape terrorism coverage from inside the major TV and radio networks.

Analysts have been wooed in hundreds of private briefings with senior military leaders, including officials with significant influence over contracting and budget matters, records show. They have been taken on tours of Iraq and given access to classified intelligence. They have been briefed by officials from the White House, State Department and Justice Department, including Mr. Cheney, Alberto R. Gonzales and Stephen J. Hadley.

In turn, members of this group have echoed administration talking points, sometimes even when they suspected the information was false or inflated. Some analysts acknowledge they suppressed doubts because they feared jeopardizing their access.

A few expressed regret for participating in what they regarded as an effort to dupe the American public with propaganda dressed as independent military analysis.

This article can be read in its entirety at
http://www.nytimes.com/2008/04/20/washington/20generals.html?_r=2 &hp&oref=slogin&oref=slogin As of 5/26/08

THE BIG WHIG FRAUD

In 2002, the Bush administration set up an information group called WHIG (White House Iraq Group). This group was to set up and guide the propaganda campaign for a war against Iraq by 2003. The group was put together in August of 2002 by White House Chief of Staff Andrew Card and Karl Rove. The goal was to market a war against Iraq to the American public by using escalation rhetoric. These officials were to embellish on an alleged eminent threat that Iraq purportedly posed to the United States. The Group was to scare the population by using words and phrases like "a mushroom cloud." This deception is nothing new. President Lyndon B. Johnson's administration did the same thing in 1967 concerning the Vietnam propaganda.

According to a book written by Newsweek columnist Michael Isikoff entitled; *Hubris: The Inside Story of Spin, Scandal, and the Selling of the Iraq War,* Michael Gerson, the top Bush speechwriter, proposed the use of a "Smoking gun" and "Mushroom cloud" metaphors to sell to the public. This gave the impression that Iraq posed a nuclear threat to the United States and its allies.

> *"The original plan had been to place it in an upcoming presidential speech, but WHIG members fancied it so much that when the Times reporters contacted the White House to talk about their upcoming piece [about aluminum tubes], one of them leaked Gerson's phrase—and the administration would soon make maxi-mum use of it." (Hubris, p. 35.)*

These types of propagandas and lies ruined the career of Valerie Plame. She was the CIA agent whose cover was blown by the administration because her husband, former Ambassador Joseph C. Wilson IV, wrote a piece that was published in the New York Times on July 6, 2003, entitled *"What I Didn't Find in Africa."* The article exposed the fact that the administration lied and purposely used weak, unreliable intelligence data about Iraq's intended purchase of Uranium from Africa to support the pre-emptive, unprovoked war against Iraq. I do not know what needs to be done, or what needs to happen in order for the public to understand that these people are criminals. They make the Mafia look like law abiding citizens. If you think these demons are in office to protect your rights, you probably need a psychiatrist.

Is it still a conspiracy theory when they lay it all out for you? This is the New York Times and other publications exposing the fact that the War on Terror is a fraud. Are the New York Times and Washington Post partaking in conspiracy theories? Do you understand what is going on around you? The government hires analyst to appear on television to promote their war agendas. Meanwhile, the same analyst were helping the defense contractors get multi-million dollar deals with the government. Are we out to lunch or what?

The Washington Post

Records Could Shed Light on Iraq Group

By Walter Pincus

Monday, June 9, 2008; Page A15

Members of the White House Iraq Group in 2002 included Condoleezza Rice, Karen Hughes and Andrew H. Card Jr. (By Pablo Martinez Monsivais -- Associated Press)

Members of the White House Iraq Group in 2002 included Condoleezza Rice, Karen Hughes and Andrew H. Card Jr. (By Pablo Martinez Monsivais -- Associated Press)

There is an important line in last week's Senate intelligence committee report on the Bush administration's prewar exaggerations of the threat posed by Saddam Hussein. It says that the panel did not review "less formal communications between intelligence agencies and other parts of the Executive Branch."

More important, there was no effort to obtain White House records or interview President Bush, Vice President Cheney or other administration officials whose speeches were analyzed because, the report says, such steps were considered beyond the scope of the report.

One obvious target for such an expanded inquiry would have been the records of the White House Iraq Group (WHIG), a group set up in August 2002 by then-White House Chief of Staff Andrew H. Card Jr.

The group met weekly in the Situation Room. Among the regular participants (many have since left or changed jobs) were Karl Rove, the president's senior political adviser; communications strategists Karen Hughes, Mary Matalin and James R. Wilkinson; legislative liaison Nicholas E. Calio; and policy aides led by national security adviser Condoleezza Rice and her deputy, Stephen J. Hadley, as well as I. Lewis "Scooter" Libby, Cheney's chief of staff.

As former White House press secretary Scott McClellan wrote in his recently released book, "What Happened," the Iraq Group "had been set up in the summer of 2002 to coordinate the marketing of the war to the public."

"The script had been finalized with great care over the summer," McClellan wrote, for a "campaign to convince Americans that war with Iraq was inevitable and necessary."

In an interview with the New York Times published Sept. 6, 2002, Card did not mention the group, but he hinted at its mission. "From a marketing point of view, you don't introduce new products in August," he said.

Two days later, WHIG's product placement was on display. It began with a front-page story in the Times describing Iraq's clandestine purchase of aluminum tubes that, the story said, could be used to produce weapons-grade uranium. The story said that information came from "senior administration officials."

The story also spoke of "hardliners" in the Bush administration being "alarmed that American intelligence underestimated the pace and scale of Iraq's nuclear program before Baghdad's defeat in the gulf war." They "argue that Washington dare not wait until analysts have found hard evidence that Mr. Hussein has acquired a nuclear weapon. The first sign of a 'smoking gun,' they argue, may be a mushroom cloud," the Times story said.

That same morning, the message was carried on three network news shows. Cheney appeared on NBC's "Meet the Press" and, referring to the Times story, said that intelligence showed that Hussein "has reconstituted his nuclear program to develop a nuclear weapon." The Iraqi leader was "trying, through his illicit procurement network, to acquire the equipment he needs to be able to enrich uranium to make the bombs," Cheney said.

That same day, on CNN's "Late Edition," Rice said, "There will always be some uncertainty" in determining how close Iraq may be to obtaining a nuclear weapon but, "we don't want the smoking gun to be a mushroom cloud."

On CBS's "Face the Nation," Defense Secretary Donald H. Rumsfeld was asked about the Times story and whether Hussein had nuclear weapons. "Is there a smoking gun here?" host Bob Schieffer asked. " 'Smoking gun' is an interesting phrase," Rumsfeld said, and then he went to the same message his colleagues had given.

"The problem with that is the way one gains absolute certainty as to whether a dictator like Saddam Hussein has a nuclear weapon is if he uses it . . . and that's a little late." Bush picked up the slogan a month later in his nationally televised speech on the threat from Iraq.

McClellan wrote that WHIG was not used to "deliberately mislead the public" but that the "more fundamental problem was the way [Bush's] advisers decided to pursue a political propaganda campaign to sell the war to the American people.

"As the campaign accelerated," he added, "caveats and qualifications were downplayed or dropped altogether. Contradictory intelligence was largely ignored or simply disregarded."

WHIG's records would shed much light on whether, as Sen. John D. Rockefeller IV (D-W.Va.), chairman of the intelligence panel, put it: "In making the case for war, the administration repeatedly presented intelligence as fact when it was unsubstantiated, contradicted or even nonexistent."

This article can be found at: http://www.washingtonpost.com/wp-dyn/content/article/2008/06/08/AR2008060801819.html

The propaganda blitz was already taking place on 9/11. Who can forget the dancing Palestinians? Do you remember the joy and dancing on the streets? Americans were told that these people were celebrating the attacks. Later it was discovered that Israeli reporters staged those scenes. Annette Krüger Spitta of ARD's (German public broadcasting) TV magazine *Panorama* stated that inspection of the unreleased complete tape shows the street around the celebration was quiet and a man in a white T-shirt was noticeable for inciting the children and fetching new people again and again. The woman who is remembered for her cheering (Nowel Abdel Fatah) later stated she was offered cake if she celebrated on camera. At the time Ms. Nowel Abdel Fatah was unaware of the 9/11 Terror Attacks. She became frightened, upon viewing pictures on television that portrayed the celebrating in a negative light.

Meanwhile, back at the ranch, a straw man theory of the dancing Palestinians was being purposely rumored. This rumor stipulated that the footage of the dancing Palestinians was ten years old. The rumor was allegedly started via e-mail by Márcio Carvalho, a student from the State University of Campinas in Brazil. He claimed one of his professors had videotapes from 1991 proving CNN misled its viewers. The professor allegedly complained to CNN and other news organizations about it. After the rumor spread, the stage was set. All the focus was on whether the tapes were ten years old. This took the focus off of the "cake offering" and the fact that Israeli cameramen were deceiving the public. After the straw man rumor about the ten year old footage was dispelled, the fraudsters were in the clear.

Note: Some or part of the following article may be grammatically incorrect because it was translated from the German language using the Google translator.

The power of TV images
What is the truth?
By Lisa Erdmann

Only a few hours after the attacks on New York and Washington showed the world's television pictures of Palestinians, the incredible fact bejubelten. Now it is a part of these images may be, the rest of age.

AP

Jubilation in front of the camera for a piece of cake

Hamburg - cheering children, a woman with a black headscarf and glasses joyful tears the arms high, a man slaps and other beckons passers herbei: A street scene, filmed in Jerusalem on 11 September, on the day of the attacks in New York and Washington. Images that went around the world. Pictures, which many people shaken. The hunger for information and footage was insatiable on that day - even these were records of the TV channels over and over again sent, accompanied by the words, this would be the Palestinian attacks in the United States celebrate. But now, ten days after the attacks, reported the ARD Politmagazin "Panorama" that it might be another truth about these pictures, that the scene might even asked.

Gefilmt were cheering Palestinians from two news agencies, Reuters and the Associated Press (AP). The viewers got in the last week only a few seconds of the material to see. Overall, ran to the TV stations but about four minutes. The Panorama editor Annette Kruger Spitta led the entire tapes of the two agencies need. "This is finally explosive material". It inconsistencies in it.

The ready-cut messages movies in the past week had the impression that because many people celebrated in the streets. There were no total shots in the process showed the entire street, but only small groups of people. On the supplied material, however, were very well shot

AP

Children celebrate in front of the camera the attacks - in the background innocent passers-by to rush

- they clearly showed that only a handful of Palestinians cheered, and many others were simply unbeteiligt over. "The woman with the headscarf has subsequently said that it had gejubelt into the camera, because you promised her cake," said Kruger Spitta. The Palestinian have said they had been horrified when she saw the context in which their jubilation was shown. They hate the deeds in New York and Washington. What is the truth?

Article can be found and read in full at:
http://translate.google.com/translate?hl=en&sl=du&u=http://www.wtc-trauer.de/mirror/Spiegel_DieMachtderTVBilder.htm

CNN and other news outlets showed the celebrating Palestinians without interviewing a single one. No Palestinian went on record to state they were indeed celebrating the attacks. The airing was obviously a propaganda piece that received far more coverage than the five dancing Israelis who were caught filming and celebrating the World Trade Center attacks from atop a white van. Had these five men been of Arab decent, they would not have been released. ABC News reported that when the police stopped the men in the white van, one of the men was quoted as saying "We are Israeli. We are not your problem. Your problems are our problems. The Palestinians are the problem." ABC News also reported the white van was owned by an Israeli company named Urban Moving. This company was reported to have had ties to Israeli intelligence, and was serving as a cover for an Israeli intelligence operation. In addition, the owner of the Urban Moving Company moved back to Israel immediately after being interviewed by the FBI. The owner left in such a hurry that he left office equipment and some of his client's property lying around in the warehouse.

Were Israelis Detained on Sept. 11 Spies?

Were Israelis Detained on Sept. 11 Spies?
June 21, 2002

Millions saw the horrific images of the World Trade Center attacks, and those who saw them won't forget them. But a New Jersey homemaker saw something that morning that prompted an investigation into five young Israelis and their possible connection to Israeli intelligence. Maria, who asked us not to use her last name, had a view of the World Trade Center from her New Jersey apartment building. She remembers a neighbor calling her shortly after the first plane hit the towers. She grabbed her binoculars and watched the destruction unfolding in lower Manhattan. But as she watched the disaster, something else caught her eye. Maria says she saw three young men kneeling on the roof of a white van in the parking lot of her apartment building. "They seemed to be taking a movie," Maria said. The men were taking video or photos of themselves with the World Trade Center burning in the background, she said. What struck Maria were the expressions on the men's faces. "They were like happy, you

know ... They didn't look shocked to me. I thought it was very strange,"
she said.

She found the behavior so suspicious that she wrote down the license
plate number of the van and called the police. Before long, the FBI was
also on the scene, and a statewide bulletin was issued on the van. The
plate number was traced to a van owned by a company called Urban
Moving. Around 4 p.m. on Sept. 11, the van was spotted on a service
road off Route 3, near New Jersey's Giants Stadium. A police officer
pulled the van over, finding five men, between 22 and 27 years old, in
the vehicle. The men were taken out of the van at gunpoint and
handcuffed by police. The arresting officers said they saw a lot that
aroused their suspicion about the men. One of the passengers had
$4,700 in cash hidden in his sock. Another was carrying two foreign
passports. A box cutter was found in the van. But perhaps the biggest
surprise for the officers came when the five men identified themselves
as Israeli citizens.

'We Are Not Your Problem'

According to the police report, one of the passengers told the officers
they had been on the West Side Highway in Manhattan "during the
incident" — referring to the World Trade Center attack. The driver of
the van, Sivan Kurzberg, told the officers, "We are Israeli. We are not
your problem. Your problems are our problems. The Palestinians are
the problem." The other passengers were his brother Paul Kurzberg,
Yaron Shmuel, Oded Ellner and Omer Marmari. When the men were
transferred to jail, the case was transferred out of the FBI's Criminal
Division, and into the bureau's Foreign Counterintelligence Section,
which is responsible for espionage cases, ABCNEWS has learned.

One reason for the shift, sources told ABCNEWS, was that the FBI
believed Urban Moving may have been providing cover for an Israeli
intelligence operation. After the five men were arrested, the FBI got a
warrant and searched Urban Moving's Weehawken, N.J., offices. The
FBI searched Urban Moving's offices for several hours, removing
boxes of documents and a dozen computer hard drives. The FBI also
questioned Urban Moving's owner. His attorney insists that his client
answered all of the FBI's questions. But when FBI agents tried to
interview him again a few days later, he was gone.

Three months later 2020's cameras photographed the inside of Urban
Moving, and it looked as if the business had been shut down in a big

hurry. Cell phones were lying around; office phones were still connected; and the property of dozens of clients remained in the warehouse.
The owner had also cleared out of his New Jersey home, put it up for sale and returned with his family to Israel.

'A Scary Situation'

Steven Gordon, the attorney for the five Israeli detainees, acknowledged that his clients' actions on Sept. 11 would easily have aroused suspicions. "You got a group of guys that are taking pictures, on top of a roof, of the World Trade Center. They're speaking in a foreign language. They got two passports on 'em. One's got a wad of cash on him, and they got box cutters. Now that's a scary situation."
But Gordon insisted that his clients were just five young men who had come to America for a vacation, ended up working for a moving company, and were taking pictures of the event.

The five Israelis were held at the Metropolitan Detention Center in Brooklyn, ostensibly for overstaying their tourist visas and working in the United States illegally. Two weeks after their arrest, an immigration judge ordered them to be deported. But sources told ABCNEWS that FBI and CIA officials in Washington put a hold on the case. The five men were held in detention for more than two months. Some of them were placed in solitary confinement for 40 days, and some of them were given as many as seven lie-detector tests. Plenty of Speculation Since their arrest, plenty of speculation has swirled about the case, and what the five men were doing that morning. Eventually, The Forward, a respected Jewish newspaper in New York, reported the FBI concluded that two of the men were Israeli intelligence operatives. Vince Cannistraro, a former chief of operations for counterterrorism with the CIA who is now a consultant for ABCNEWS, said federal authorities' interest in the case was heightened when some of the men's names were found in a search of a national intelligence database. Israeli Intelligence Connection?

According to Cannistraro, many people in the U.S. intelligence community believed that some of the men arrested were working for Israeli intelligence. Cannistraro said there was speculation as to whether Urban Moving had been "set up or exploited for the purpose of launching an intelligence operation against radical Islamists in the area, particularly in the New Jersey-New York area." Under this scenario, the alleged spying operation was not aimed against the

United States, but at penetrating or monitoring radical fund-raising and support networks in Muslim communities like Paterson, N.J., which was one of the places where several of the hijackers lived in the months prior to Sept. 11. For the FBI, deciphering the truth from the five Israelis proved to be difficult. One of them, Paul Kurzberg, refused to take a lie-detector test for 10 weeks — then failed it, according to his lawyer. Another of his lawyers told us Kurzberg had been reluctant to take the test because he had once worked for Israeli intelligence in another country.

Sources say the Israelis were targeting these fund-raising networks because they were thought to be channeling money to Hamas and Islamic Jihad, groups that are responsible for most of the suicide bombings in Israel. "[The] Israeli government has been very concerned about the activity of radical Islamic groups in the United States that could be a support apparatus to Hamas and Islamic Jihad," Cannistraro said. The men denied that they had been working for Israeli intelligence out of the New Jersey moving company, and Ram Horvitz, their Israeli attorney, dismissed the allegations as "stupid and ridiculous." Mark Regev, the spokesman for the Israeli Embassy in Washington, goes even further, asserting the issue was never even discussed with U.S. officials. "These five men were not involved in any intelligence operation in the United States, and the American intelligence authorities have never raised this issue with us," Regev said. "The story is simply false."

No 'Pre-Knowledge'

Despite the denials, sources tell ABCNEWS there is still debate within the FBI over whether or not the young men were spies. Many U.S. government officials still believe that some of them were on a mission for Israeli intelligence. But the FBI told ABCNEWS, "To date, this investigation has not identified anybody who in this country had pre-knowledge of the events of 9/11." Sources also said that even if the men were spies, there is no evidence to conclude they had advance knowledge of the terrorist attacks on Sept. 11. The investigation, at the end of the day, after all the polygraphs, all of the field work, all the cross-checking, the intelligence work, concluded that they probably did not have advance knowledge of 9/11," Cannistraro noted.

As to what they were doing on the van, they say they read about the attack on the Internet, couldn't see it from their offices and went to the parking lot for a better view. But no one has been able to find a good explanation for why they may have been smiling with the towers of the World Trade Center burning in the background. Both the lawyers for the young men and the Israeli Embassy chalk it up to immature conduct. According to ABCNEWS sources, Israeli and U.S. government officials worked out a deal — and after 71 days, the five Israelis were taken out of jail, put on a plane, and deported back home. While the former detainees refused to answer ABCNEWS' questions about their detention and what they were doing on Sept. 11, several of the detainees discussed their experience in America on an Israeli talk show after their return home. Said one of the men, denying that they were laughing or happy on the morning of Sept. 11, "The fact of the matter is we are coming from a country that experiences terror daily. Our purpose was to document the event."

ABCNEWS' Chris Isham, John Miller, Glenn Silber and Chris Vlasto contributed to this report.

This article can be views at
http://abcnews.go.com/2020/Story?id=123885&page=1 as of 9/8/08

The Israeli Government and the five dancing Israelis claimed that they were there to "document the event." A very serious question arises from that statement. If there was no prior knowledge of the attacks, how could their purpose have been to document the event? If I am misinterpreting what they meant by that statement, what the heck are movers doing with a video camera filming the attacks? Why would the woman, who called the authorities, lie about witnessing the men celebrating?

If you are getting the impression that Israel was behind the 9/11 Terror Attacks, that is not my intention. Albeit, I do not doubt that the Mossad (Israel intelligence) had a hand in the attacks. One thing is certain, the 9/11 terror plot was much deeper than just the Mossad or the CIA. There were many hands in the cookie jar. We have been deceived big time.

They were playing with our emotions from the first instance. They had everyone waving flags and putting them on the antennas of their cars, not realizing that the criminals who run Washington are the biggest anti-American promoters on the planet. You had George W. Bush saying the terrorists hate our freedoms on one hand, and then obliterating sections of the Bill of Rights with the passing of the Patriot Act on the other hand. Most people do not know that the term "USA Patriot" is actually an Acronym. It stands for "**U**niting and **S**trengthening **A**merica by **P**roviding **A**ppropriate **T**ools **R**equired to **I**ntercept and **O**bstruct **T**errorism." This is a clever way to make you psychologically believe that if you are against the Act, you are not a patriot. Of course though, the Act has little to do with the bogus War on Terror. The real war is against you! Wake up! These demons are now arresting people under the Act for a simple marijuana joint. Do you understand that? If you smoke marijuana, you are a terrorist now. If you take a picture of a politician (a public servant), you may be arrested for terrorism.

We need to understand how incredible these anti-terror laws really are. Hitler and Stalin did not even pass these types of laws. They just did their devilishment. How ruthless and gangster are the criminals in Washington to actually put this stuff on paper? It becomes lawful for them to violate your inalienable rights, all in the name of protecting the very same rights they are violating.

How can they make it lawful to break the law? They have created checkpoints in train stations and bus terminals with police officers asking to search your bags. If you comply and do not object to the police checking your bags, then you have waived your Fourth Amendment rights. If you object and they threaten you with arrest or any other form of coercion, they are in violation of your constitutional rights and are subject to being sued. The people's right to not be unreasonably searched (unless there is probable cause that you have, or will commit a crime) cannot be violated!

UNITED STATES CONSTITUTION

Amendment IV: *The right of the people to be secure in their persons, houses, papers, and effects, against unreasonable **searches** and seizures**, shall not be violated**; and no warrants shall issue, but upon probable cause, supported by oath or affirmation, and particularly the place to be searched, and the persons or things to be seized.*

Photographer Arrested "Under Patriot Act"

posted by md on Sunday December 08, @09:35PM
from the dept.

A number of alternative online news outlets, namely 2600 Magazine, and more recently Declan McCullagh's Politech are carrying a story of a Denver photographer who was apparently arrested while taking pictures in Denver, during Vice President Dick Cheney's visit to the city. Denver resident Mike Maginnis reports being physically assaulted by Denver police, and then held for hours while being verbally assaulted by men who represented themselves as federal agents working for the Secret Service. The latter, Maginnis claims, threatened to charge him as a "terrorist" under the USA Patriot Act.

Maginnis apparently tried to phone a Denver area newspaper, only to have his phone call disconnected when authorities discovered who he was contacting. No doubt, this is only a small taste of what's to come from the USA Patriot act and other bang-up efforts at defending the U.S. against terrorism.

Source: http://grep.law.harvard.edu/articles/02/12/08/2244247.shtml

---

patriot act used to arrest environmental activists

December 15, 2005 2:45 PM   Subscribe

Patriot Act used to arrest environmental activists

"Federal marshals arrested six environmental activists in a series of coordinated raids in four states yesterday, Dec. 8, in apparent response to a string of arsons in Oregon and Washington attributed to the Earth Liberation Front (ELF)" ... has the patriot act produced any arrests in the country related to 9-11?

posted by specialk420 (105 comments total)

Source: http://www.metafilter.com/47637/patriot-act-used-to-arrest-environmental-activists

MAN CHARGED UNDER PATRIOT ACT IN LASER CASE

Wednesday, January 05, 2005

NEWARK, N.J. — A man charged with temporarily blinding the pilot and co-pilot of an airplane with a laser beam claims he was simply using the device to look at stars with his 7-year-old daughter.

*Federal authorities Tuesday used the **Patriot Act (search)** to charge **David Banach (search)**, 38, with interfering with the operator of a mass transportation vehicle and making false statements to the FBI. He is the first person arrested after a recent rash of reports around the nation of laser beams hitting airplanes.*

The FBI acknowledged the incident had no connection to terrorism but called Banach's actions "foolhardy and negligent."

Source: http://www.foxnews.com/story/0,2933,143371,00.html

I know that the following piece of information may not mean much to you right now, but this is an astronomical victory for us common folk. This goes to show that the devils in Washington can be put in their place.

STATE OF OKLAHOMA
2nd Session of the 51st Legislature (2008)
HOUSE JOINT RESOLUTION 1089 By: Key
AS INTRODUCED
A Joint Resolution claiming sovereignty under the Tenth Amendment to the Constitution of the United States over certain powers; serving notice to the federal government to cease and desist certain mandates; and directing distribution.

WHEREAS, the Tenth Amendment to the Constitution of the United States reads as follows: "The powers not delegated to the United States by the Constitution, nor prohibited by it to the States, are reserved to the States respectively, or to the people."; and

WHEREAS, the Tenth Amendment defines the total scope of federal power as being that specifically granted by the Constitution of the United States and no more; and

WHEREAS, the scope of power defined by the Tenth Amendment means that the federal government was created by the states specifically to be an agent of the states; and

WHEREAS, today, in 2008, the states are demonstrably treated as agents of the federal government; and

WHEREAS, many federal mandates are directly in violation of the Tenth Amendment to the Constitution of the United States; and

WHEREAS, the United States Supreme Court has ruled in New York v. United States, 112 S. Ct. 2408 (1992), that Congress may not simply commandeer the legislative and regulatory processes of the states; and

WHEREAS, a number of proposals from previous administrations and some now pending from the present administration and from Congress may further violate the Constitution of the United States. **NOW, THEREFORE, BE IT RESOLVED BY THE HOUSE OF REPRESENTATIVES AND THE SENATE OF THE 2ND SESSION OF THE 51ST OKLAHOMA LEGISLATURE:** THAT the State of Oklahoma hereby claims sovereignty under the Tenth Amendment to the Constitution of the United States over all powers not otherwise enumerated and granted to the federal government by the Constitution of the United States. THAT this serve as Notice and Demand to the federal government, as our agent, to cease and desist, effective immediately, mandates that are beyond the scope of these constitutionally delegated powers.

THAT a copy of this resolution be distributed to the President of the United States, the President of the United States Senate, the Speaker of the United States House of Representatives, the Speaker of the House and the President of the Senate of each state's legislature of the United States of America, and each member of the Oklahoma Congressional Delegation.

Sources:
http://www.okhouse.gov/51LEG/Leg_Votesxx.aspx?include=okh01983.txt
http://www.ok-safe.com/files/documents/1/HJR1089_int.pdf

This is a tremendous victory. In short, it means that unconstitutional laws—such as the Patriot Act—will not apply in Oklahoma. The resolution correctly puts the federal government in its proper place. The State of Oklahoma put the District of Columbia (Washington) on notice of their contractual (constitutional) obligation as an agent of the fifty states. As an agent of the fifty states, the federal government's purpose is to serve those states. Today, it is the total opposite. Do we understand that? Do we know what the purpose of our federal government is? It is a shame that most people do not have a clue as to what the role of the federal government is supposed to be. It is the same ignorance that has the people serving the government, instead of the government serving the people. Does the term "PUBLIC SERVANT" mean anything?

The government's only purpose is to secure your right to life, liberty, and the pursuit of happiness. If the government does anything outside of that function, the government is out of order. If you do not object and put the government back in its place, then you are out of order. This is what has happened throughout the whole planet. The Unknowns have played to your ignorance of what the role of government is supposed to be. The government has you believing that they are above you. They have you believing that they have the authority to tell you what to do. You are under the impression that they have the authority to issue you licenses. According to Black's Law Dictionary, Eight Edition, a license is a permission to do something that would otherwise be illegal. Can you smell the fraud of having licenses? But of course, they had to convince you to acquiesce (waive your rights) and allow them to run the scam of licenses. They succeeded by telling you that if the doctors, nurses, lawyers, drivers, and so on are licensed, you will be protected. They always have to make you believe that they have your best interest in mind. However, if I want to be a doctor, having to obtain a license is an obstruction to my pursuit of happiness. Therefore, they are no longer acting in a governmental capacity. Their only role is to make sure that your right to life, liberty, and the pursuit of happiness is not infringed upon. However, the government may only step in after your rights have been violated, not before. The

United States Government was set up to be reactive, not pro-active.

Declaration of Independence (in part)

In CONGRESS, July 4, 1776
The unanimous Declaration of the thirteen united States of America

When in the Course of human events it becomes necessary for one people to dissolve the political bands which have connected them with another and to assume among the powers of the earth, the separate and equal station to which the Laws of Nature and of Nature's God entitle them, a decent respect to the opinions of mankind requires that they should declare the causes which impel them to the separation.

We hold these truths to be self-evident, that all men are created equal, that they are endowed by their Creator with <u>certain unalienable Rights, that among these are Life, Liberty and the pursuit of Happiness.</u> — That to secure these rights, Governments are instituted among Men, deriving their just powers from the consent of the governed,</u> — That whenever any Form of Government becomes destructive of these ends, it is the Right of the People to alter or to abolish it, and to institute new Government, laying its foundation on such principles and organizing its powers in such form, as to them shall seem most likely to effect their Safety and Happiness. Prudence, indeed, will dictate that Governments long established should not be changed for light and transient causes; and accordingly <u>all experience hath shewn that mankind are more disposed to suffer, while evils are sufferable than to right themselves by abolishing the forms to which they are accustomed.</u> But when a long train of abuses and usurpations, pursuing invariably the same Object evinces a design to reduce them under absolute Despotism, it is their right, it is their duty, to throw off such Government, and to provide new Guards for their future security…..

Source: http://www.ushistory.org/Declaration/document/index.htm

2

THE UNKNOWNS

The few who rule the many are called by numerous names. Most of us make the mistake of giving them a single face and then concluding that once we take down that face, our lives will be better. To the contrary, the few have their hands on every government, race, religion, secret society, nationality, political party, and what ever else you can think of. They put one against the other while supporting both sides. You will never see them, hear them, or know their names. They are much too intelligent for that. Again, it is important to note that it is not any particular group. They are virtually unknown by name or appearance. I do not try to label these devils because doing so would be futile. Therefore, within these pages they will be referred to as the "Unknown Traitors" or simply as "The Unknowns." I know that there are those who are already saying to themselves, "Oh no, another conspiracy nut." However, take a look at what some people with so-called authority and power had to say about the Unknowns.

On November 21, 1933, President Franklin Roosevelt wrote a letter to Colonel Edward Mandell House, President Woodrow Wilson's close advisor, in where he state;

"The real truth of the matter is, as you and I know, that a financial element in the larger centers has owned the government every since the days of Andrew Jackson..."

Franklin Delano Roosevelt

The fact that there exists a cabal of power brokers controlling governments from behind the scenes has been detailed several times by credible sources. Professor Carroll Quigley, President Bill Clinton's mentor at Georgetown University, wrote a book entitled *Tragedy and Hope* (1966), in which he states:

"There does exist and has existed for a generation, an international...network which operates, to some extent, in the way the radical right believes the Communists act. In fact, this network, which we may identify as the Round Table Groups, has no aversion to cooperating with the Communists, or any other groups and frequently does so. I know of the operations of this network because I have studied it for twenty years and was permitted for two years, in the early 1960s, to examine its papers and secret

records. I have no aversion to it or to most of its aims and have, for much of my life, been close to it and to many of its instruments. I have objected, both in the past and recently, to a few of its policies...but in general my chief difference of opinion is that it wishes to remain unknown, and I believe its role in history is significant enough to be known."

(Professor Carroll Quigley)

Quigley also states, "Classes of early Rhodes Scholars were responsible for introducing South African apartheid." As for the United States, Quigley writes of how Paul Warburg, the architect of the Bank of Socialist Germany, was quietly brought into the United States to form our national banking system. He is making reference to the Federal Reserve Bank; which is neither federal, nor does it have any reserves. The system was set up to maintain direct connections to the Bank of England, the Bank of France, and the Bank of Germany. These demons who work behind the scenes have captured every particle of the United States Government. This sentiment was also accepted to be true by high ranking Judicial Officers.

United States Supreme Court Justice Felix Frankfurter Stated, *"The real rulers in Washington are invisible and exercise power from behind the scenes."* Whether consciously or by mere happenstance, Justice Frankfurt had certain associations with the criminal elite. Despite the fact that he was raised in a poor Jewish neighborhood, his academic credentials earned him entrance into the world of the eastern intellectual elite. In 1919, he became a Zionist delegate to the Paris Peace

Conference. He also played a major role in the foundation of the American Civil Liberties Union, most commonly known as the ACLU. Today the ACLU is used to defame and discredit anyone who attacks the current system of control (slavery).

U.S. Supreme Court Justice Felix Frankfurter

The twenty-eighth President of the United States, Woodrow Wilson, stated: "The *government, which was designed for the people, has got into the hands of the bosses and their employers, the special interests. An invisible empire has been set up above the forms of democracy.*" When these men are elected to the highest positions of power, the people believe that the buck stops with them. However, that could not be further from the truth. Certainly, whenever a member of the criminal elite gets defamed or ousted, it is because they have done something that has gone against the agenda or status quo of the Unknowns.

The average person may not have any understanding of the Unknowns. Nevertheless, powerful men such as presidents, Supreme Court Justices, professors, and others in positions of power have repeatedly warned about another power above theirs.

President Woodrow Wilson

In 1913, prior to the passage of the Federal Reserve Act, President Wilson's *The New Freedom* was published, in which he revealed; *"Since I entered politics, I have chiefly had men's views confided to me privately. Some of the biggest men in the U. S., in the field of commerce and manufacturing, are afraid of somebody, are afraid of something. They know that there is a power somewhere so organized, so subtle, so watchful, so interlocked, so complete, so pervasive, that they had better not speak above their breath when they speak in condemnation of it."*

If you have heard of the Illuminati Order and thought it was some kind of mythological conspiracy theory, you are wrong. The writings of George Washington himself prove not only their (Illuminati) existence, but that they were intensively active in the United States of America. George Washington was also certain that the Illuminati had infiltrated some of the American lodges of freemasonry. The Illuminati apologists have made an effort to convince the ignorant masses that Illuminati's was disbanded in 1790. The following letter written by President Washington was in response to the concerns of a reverend named G. W. Snyder. Reverend Snyder had forwarded a copy of a book about the nefarious motives of the Illuminati Order to President George Washington—asking of his opinion.

Mount Vernon, October 24, 1798

Revd Sir: I have your favor of the 17th. instant before me; and my only motive to trouble you with the receipt of this letter, is to explain, and correct a mistake which I perceive the hurry in which I am obliged, often, to write letters, have led you into. It was not my intention to doubt that__, the Doctrines of the Illuminati__, and principles of Jacobinism__ had not spread in the United States. On the contrary, no one is more truly satisfied of this fact than I am. The idea that I meant to convey, was, that I did not believe that the Lodges of Free Masons in this Country had, as Societies, endeavored to propagate the diabolical tenets of the first, or pernicious principles of the latter (if they are susceptible of separation). That Individuals of them may have done it, or that the founder, or instrument employed to found, the __Democratic Societies__ in the United States, may have had these objects; and actually had __a separation of the People from their Government__ in view, __is too evident to be questioned__.

Source: **Washington, George, 1732-1799. The writings of George Washington from the original manuscript sources** Electronic Text Center, University of Virginia Library

Notice how the letter mentions the Democratic Societies. The so-called founding fathers knew that a democracy would separate the people from their government. This is why they set up a constitutional republic as the only form of government. A democracy is an ideal form of government for the Unknowns because it stipulates the majority rules. This sounds good on the outside. However, all you have to do is manipulate the majority. Once the majority has been manipulated, then they can do whatever they want to oppress any minority group that may be in disagreement. In contrast, a constitutional republic is that in which the majority rule is tempered by minority rights that are protected by law (Scheb, John M., An Introduction to the American Legal System, Thomson Delmar Learning 2001. p6). This is no longer the case in the United States. If the majority of the people are scammed into accepting a law, the minority who oppose get fined or thrown in jail for objecting and denouncing the law. Examples are paying personal income tax, forced participation in the social security fraud, forced licenses, forced vaccinations, and the coming carbon tax due to the global warming fraud. Those are just a few.

Getting back to the Unknowns, notice in the letter that George Washington clearly states of how the Illuminati were present here in the United States in 1798. The letter was written eight years after the alleged disbandment of the Illuminati Order. The first President of the United States acknowledged that the Illuminati were alive and well. He also stated that, although he did not believe American freemasonry as a whole was affected by the Illuminati, he was certain that there were some individuals who had been tapped. These are the individuals who are responsible for the creation of the Democratic Party, which traces its origins to the Democratic-Republican Party founded by Thomas Jefferson, James Madison, and many other influential opponents of the Federalist Party during the 1790s. George Washington said their (the Democrats and Republicans) goal was to separate the people from their government. This is exactly what has happened here in the United States. Nowadays, citizens fear their government. So much so, that those who read this documentary, and believe me to be just another conspiracy nut, will still suppose that the government could kill or imprison me for writing it. But if everything is hunky-dory and there is no conspiracy, why would the government care about what a nut like me says or writes?

As you would expect, because I am not an insider or government source, people will feel compelled to call me a conspiracy theorist. It is a wonder as to why the media and the so-called historians do not refer to the previously mentioned men as conspiracy theorist? Why is it that every time a simpleton like me expresses concern about the possibility of a conspiracy, I automatically must be a "conspiracy theorist" and an idiot? Who set up this current system, whereby, the people you are trying to warn and teach are the very same people who put up the most resistance against you? The average person will refuse to dialogue and get an understanding of the information being put in front of them. The people are on automatic mode. They believe that because they were not taught this information in school, or because the media outlets are not covering these subjects, they cannot be true.

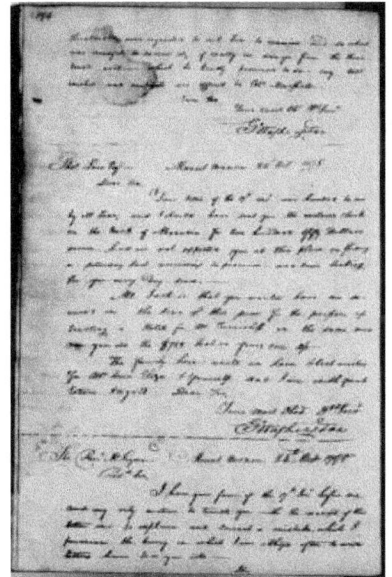

George Washington's letter to Rev. G. W. Snyder

THE BILDERBERG GROUP

For many years, people who spoke about a group known as "the Bilderbergs" were ridiculed and laughed at by news reporters. The news media's rebuttal to the existence of the Bilderberg group was, "If all these powerful people from all over the globe are gathering once a year from politicians, heads of state, banking, and large corporations etc., we would know about it." Now that the group's existence has been well documented, the tune has changed. Now the rebuttal is that this group meets to come up with better solutions to solve world problems, but they are not meeting to take it over. The question becomes, why are the meetings still held in secret? Why doesn't the mainstream media cover the event? Could you imagine if 130 movie stars or 130 professional athletes met in secret? The media would go crazy to try and get the scoop. How is it that there is no interest in a gathering of world leaders who meet in secret?

In 2003, the Bilderberg Conference occurred in Versailles, France. Surprisingly, the conference was reported by the British Broadcasting Corp. (BBC) news website in a short piece titled, "Elite Power Brokers' Secret Talks" by Emma Jane Kirby. "By anyone's standards, it is a bit of a mystery," the BBC's Kirby wrote about Bilderberg. "With its meetings Cloaked in secrecy, it is unclear what Bilderberg actually does." She also wrote, "It is an extremely influential lobbying group with a good deal of political clout on both sides of the Atlantic."

A few years ago CNN interviewed a journalist by the name of Ron Bronson, who tried to down play the fact that the world elite meet in secrecy to discuss our future. Where is the alleged democracy in that? Mr. Bronson supposed that what you have are important people slinging ideas back and forth to each other. On May 21, 2003, The Financial Times also published a featured article mentioning Bilderberg. This goes to show that simply because the media is not covering something does not make it a fairytale.

CNN on the Bilderberg Group

The term "media coverage" or "media covering" is an interesting phrase. What are they covering, or covering up? Are they telling us something to our face? I will put that in my bag of coincidences.

One of the leading researchers on the Bilderberg group is a journalist by the name of Jim Tucker. After the 2005 Bilderberg meeting, he learned of a plan to get oil prices to record levels. Needless to say, oil prices jumped from $40 a barrel in 2005 to $70 in 2006. Where are those prices today?

The following article is from the Dallas Morning News. It reports that the Governor of Texas, Rick Perry, was scheduled to leave for the 2007 Bilderberg meeting in Istanbul, Turkey. Is this a lie? Why didn't the main stream media swarm down to Turkey to get the scoop? Do we understand the importance or affect that these meetings have on every country on the planet earth? Let me reiterate it. The top people in politics, media, science, business, and anything else you can think of, meet in secret. Why? What decisions are being made in these meetings? What policies are being formed? How is that a democracy—even by today's standards?

Perry off to secret forum in Turkey
He'll speak about federalism at elite global conference
12:00 AM CDT on Thursday, May 31, 2007
By CHRISTY HOPPE/ The Dallas Morning News
choppe@dallasnews.com

AUSTIN – Gov. Rick Perry is flying to Istanbul, Turkey, today to speak at the super-secret Bilderberg Conference, a meeting of about 130 international leaders in business, media and politics.

The Associated Press

Gov. Rick Perry leaves today for the Bilderberg Conference, an exclusive, hush-hush meeting of global leaders in business, media and politics.

The invitation-only conference was started in 1954 and named for the Dutch hotel where the conference was first held. Those who attend promise not to reveal what was discussed, security is tight, and the press and public are barred. The conference has been the subject of conspiracy theorists and even Christian groups who wonder about its influence. Robert Black, the governor's press secretary, said the governor was invited to attend and speak about state-federal relations. Mr. Black dismissed the conspiracy theories. "He's looking forward to learning the secret handshake," Mr. Black joked. He said that Mr. Perry is paying for the trip and host hotel, usually among the top in the world, out of campaign contributions from his Texans for Rick Perry committee. Previous speakers at the conference have included such GOP stalwarts as outgoing World Bank chief Paul Wolfowitz and former U.S. Defense Secretary Donald Rumsfeld. Last year, the conference was held in Ottawa, and the Toronto Star reported that it had received an unsigned press release saying that the 2006 group included David Rockefeller, Henry Kissinger, Queen Beatrix of Holland, New York Gov. George Pataki, media moguls, high-level officials from Spain and Greece, and the heads of Coca-Cola, Credit Suisse and the Royal Bank of Canada. Bilderberg chairman Etienne Davignon, a former Belgian diplomat, granted the British Broadcasting Corp. a rare interview two years ago in which he brushed aside myths surrounding the organization. "When people say this is a secret government of the world, I say that if we were a secret government of the world, we should be bloody ashamed of ourselves," Mr. Davignon said. Mr. Black said that the governor was going because he was invited. "He looks forward to talking to them about the system of federalism here in the United States," he said. Regarding the secrecy surrounding the event, Mr. Black said: "It's their conference, and I suppose they can run it anyway they want. The governor was honored that they would ask him to come speak on the American experience, and he's happy to do it. "

This year (2008) the group met in the state of Virginia, where strangely enough, Barack Obama was at a rally. What becomes even stranger, or more coincidental, is the fact that Obama snuck away from his media entourage to meet Hillary Clinton in private. Both Hillary Clinton and her hubby have been attendees at past Bilderberg meetings.

Refer to; http://www.nysun.com/new-york/pataki-joins-bilderbergs-conclave/34231/

This Hillary-Obama meeting was so unorthodox that Obama's media entourage were actually kidnapped and brought back to Chicago against their wishes. The reporters did not realize that they may have been kidnapped under federal law. Obama's communications director, Robert Gibbs, informed the media (that had boarded the plane) of Obama's absence only after the doors were shut and the plane was taking off. For all of you who think that Obama is not one of them, I do not mean to step on your toes. I mean to step on your neck! Barack Obama is the new kid on the block that they want to push on you. This character is endorsed by Zbigniew Brzezinski, who is a former head of the Council on Foreign Relations. He was also a co-founder of the Trilateral Commission. Brzezinski served under the Carter administration as National Security Advisor, playing a major role in the creation of the Mujahedeen (al-Qaeda) to combat the Russians.

In Obama's race for a United States Senate seat, not a single negative ad was run against hm. There were no negative ads during the seven-way Democratic primary, or in the general election. Perhaps not so coincidently, republican Jack Ryan unexpectedly dropped out of the race after a court unsealed embarrassing divorce documents that were highly publicized by the media. As a result, Obama faced weak Republican candidate Alan Keyes, who quickly came under attack from the media and was unable to act offensively in the campaign. Now basically untouched in these past political campaigns, Obama will likely flaunt his media-created image as a moderate Democrat capable of embracing both conservative and liberal ideals.

http://www.observer.com/2008/brzezinski-power-shouldnt-have-resigned

There is no question that, as president, Obama will continue to send our kids to foreign lands to kill or be killed in the name of fighting the bogus War on Terror. In the 2004 Democratic National Convention debates, Barrack Obama states the following:

> *"Now -- now let me be clear. Let me be clear. We have real enemies in the world. These enemies must be found. They must be pursued. And they must be defeated."*

In a March 2007 speech to the American Israel Public Affairs Committee (AIPAC), a pro-Israel lobby, he stated that the best way to stop Iran from developing nuclear weapons is through talks and diplomacy—although not ruling out military action. Obama is not ruling out military action the same way President Bush did not rule it out against Iraq. Why can't we see that Barack Obama is a fraud? He opposed the Iraq War but would not rule out preemptively attacking Iran? His opposition to the Iraq War was his top selling point during the Democratic primary elections! His campaign is controlled by the Trilateral Commission and the Council on Foreign Relations. These are the same people who control the Bush administration and pushed the Iraq War. Unless something drastic happens, Barack Obama will be the next president of the United States. He has left himself an opening to continue the "Plan for a New American Century" and go on the offensive against Iran. I am in no way, shape, or form implying that John McCain is any different or any better.

 **REUTERS**

McCain doesn't rule out preemptive war

Wed Apr 9, 2008 7:52pm EDT

WESTPORT, Conn., April 9 (Reuters) - Republican U.S. presidential candidate John McCain said on Wednesday he would not rule out launching preemptive wars against future enemies.

President George W. Bush, in launching his 2003 invasion of Iraq, said it was necessary to forestall possible future attacks from a country that was developing weapons of mass destruction.

Read the complete article at:
http://www.reuters.com/article/vcCandidateFeed7/idUSN09445024

Both parties and their candidates are controlled by the same people. No matter who wins the presidency, you will see a cabinet filled with members of the Council on Foreign Relations and the Trilateral Commission.

CNNPolitics.com

Behind the Scenes: Obama press 'hijacked' during Clinton meeting

By Chris Welch

CNN

Barack Obama was conspicuously absent when his plane took off Thursday with a gaggle of reporters inside.

WASHINGTON (CNN) -- What seemed to be a routine evening waiting for Barack Obama aboard his campaign plane turned into anything but when the cabin doors closed and the passengers were informed the aircraft would be taking off immediately -- without the candidate.

The first sign something was amiss on the Thursday flight came when the pilot told those aboard -- about 25 members of the media, a smaller group of Obama staffers and only a handful of Secret Service agents -- that everyone was on board and that the plane would be departing for Obama's hometown of Chicago, Illinois, momentarily.

The press soon noticed there were far too few people aboard for a standard campaign flight. Something was different. It's fair to say that the term "everyone" was used a bit loosely -- especially when the presumptive nominee appeared to be missing.

As the plane taxied, communications director Robert Gibbs admitted that Obama was remaining behind because he "wasn't going to be back in D.C. for a while" and had "scheduled some meetings" before he left.

Obama staffers, including Gibbs and Linda Douglass, a newly appointed senior adviser and campaign spokeswoman, didn't ask the reporters on board if they'd prefer to wait on the runway in Washington until the meetings concluded. They were going to Chicago. Without Barack Obama.

Don't Miss

* Obama, Clinton hold talks in Feinstein's living room
* Bernstein: Behind the scenes with Hillary Clinton

"I'm not going to discuss what he's going to do tonight," Gibbs added before heading up to the front of the plane, moments before wheels up from Washington Dulles International Airport in Virginia.

It was just after 9 p.m. -- just about the time, it is now known, Obama was sitting down to meet with Hillary Clinton.

◄ Watch Gibbs discuss the meeting »

For 45 minutes before departure, however, Obama's staffers gave the impression that everyone was waiting because Obama would arrive shortly.

With the plane sitting on the tarmac, staffers shot the breeze with members of the press as if nothing was amiss, though they later admitted they knew all along Obama wasn't coming.

Source: http://www.cnn.com/2008/POLITICS/06/06/btsc.welch.obama.press/

THE BOHEMIAN GROVE

Another group of elites that meet in secrecy are commonly referred to as "The Bohemian Society." This somewhat secret society is said to be of German origin. The more publicly known gatherings of the society are in California. The spot is commonly known as the Bohemian Grove.

The Bohemian Grove is a secluded campground in California's Sonoma County. It is the site of an annual two-week gathering of a highly select all-male club. Club members have included every Republican President since Calvin Coolidge. Current participants include George Bush Senior and Junior, Henry Kissinger, James Baker, and David Rockefeller. It is a virtual "who's who" of the most powerful men in business and government.

Few journalists have entered the grove and been allowed to tell their story with the exception of a few. In the late 1980s, a journalist by the name of Philip Weiss provided the most detailed inside account (of that day) in his November 1989 Spy piece. Shortly after, in the summer of 1991, Dirk Mathison, San Francisco bureau chief for People Magazine infiltrated the exclusive Bohemian Grove. Mathison alleged that elite visitors of the grove included the management of Time Warner and the owner of People Magazine—which Mathison said prevented him from telling his story.

This photo was taken in 1990. The activity shown is called the Cremation of Care ceremony.

The most famous infiltration of the grounds—or widely known exposure to date—was offered by Texas radio talk show host Alex Jones of the GCN Radio Network. Mr. Jones produced a documentary film entitled; "Dark Secrets- Inside Bohemian Grove." This film documented the first ever hidden recording of the Grove. It captured the demonic ritual called "The Cremation of Care." This is a child sacrificing ritual that is performed by select members. The footage of the film shows members worshipping Molech, an ancient Canaanite/Moabite god. It is very important that you understand who Molech was, and even more importantly, what Molech's congregation practiced.

The following article is an excerpt from Jewish Encyclopedia.com. It may still be found at the following link as of 2/29/08.

http://www.jewishencyclopedia.com/view.jsp?artid=718&letter=M

In the Masoretic text the name is "Molech"; in the Septuagint "Moloch." The earliest mention of Molech is in Lev. xviii. 21, where the Israelite is forbidden to sacrifice any of his children to Molech. Similarly, in Lev. xx. 2-5, it is enacted that a man who sacrifices his seed to Molech shall surely be put to death. Then, curiously, it is provided that he shall be cut off from the congregation. In I Kings xi. 7 it is said that Solomon built a high place for Molech in the mountain "that is before Jerusalem." The same passage calls Molech an Ammonite deity. The Septuagint as quoted in the New Testament (Acts vii. 43) finds a reference to Moloch in Amos v. 26; but this is a doubtful passage. In II Kings xxiii. 10 it is stated that one of the practises to which Josiah put a stop by his reform was that of sacrificing children to Molech, and that the place where this form of worship had been practised was at Topheth, "in the valley of the children of Hinnom." This statement is confirmed by Jer. xxxii. 35. From II Kings xxi. 6 it may be inferred that this worship was introduced during the reign of Manasseh. The impression left by an uncritical reading of these passages is that Molech-worship, with its rite of child-sacrifice, was introduced from Ammon during the seventh century B.C.

Here we have these people in positions of apparent power, performing ancient Canaanite rituals and alleging to be Christians. In the video footage obtained by Mr. Jones, you can clearly see the mock sacrifice of a child. However, one can only assume the sacrifice was mocked. The film is not steady enough to give us the information necessary to prove (without a doubt) that it was either a mock, or a real sacrifice. Either way, these are the people you defend and protect every time you disregard someone as "crazy" for attempting to point these things out. These people are not leaders. They are misleaders. They mislead you in all types of ways. One of their favorite deceptions is to make you believe they are at odds with each other, or that they disagree on ideas and thoughts. Meanwhile, behind closed doors, you have these secret meetings between people who you think are at odds with each other. As an example, Helmut Heinrich Waldemar Schmidt (born December 23, 1918) was a German Social Democratic politician and the Chancellor of West Germany from 1974 to 1982. He served as Minister of Defense, Minister of Finance and briefly also served as the Minister of Economics. In November of 2007, Schmidt wrote an article in the German weekly *Die Zeit* stating that America was a greater threat to world peace than Russia. He explained how Russia had not invaded its neighbors since the end of the Cold War. Schmidt claimed he was surprised that Russia allowed Ukraine and other former components of the Soviet Union to secede peacefully. He noted the United States' invasion of Iraq under George W. Bush was "A war of choice, not a war of necessity."

These statements are made to get the unsuspecting fools to believe there is conflict. However, Helmut Schmidt, in his own autobiography entitled *"Men and Powers, a Political Retrospective,"* admits he is a member of the Council on Foreign Relations, the Trilateral Commission, and the Bilderberg group. He admits to having been working toward bringing a one world government. In his book, Mr. Schmidt mentions that leaders who agree with the global agenda for a one world government go to the Grove every summer. He also writes about secret groves in Germany, where the members perform druidic rituals. However, he states that the Bohemian Grove in California, U.S. of A. is his favorite place to participate in the rituals.

Lakeside 1991:
Helmut Schmidt

But this global agenda is commonly known as the New World Order. Unfortunately, many of us do not really understand this term. Many believe that a new order is absolutely evil. A new order in the world is only evil if it is led by the Unknowns and their puppets. But what is the New World Order? One of the first questions that come to mind when I hear people talk about the New World Order is, "what is the old order?" If there is a new order, it is a confession that there is, or was an old order. But what was the old order? The old order controlled people by and through religion. Today, it is by way of politics, banking, and the legal system. They have to control what you think and feel in order to make you act the way they want you to act. They do this by controlling all the media outlets and the so-called educational system. What you see and read (from the time you are born) shapes your attitude as well as the way you act and think. Many of the messages are subliminal. However, for the most part, the messages are right in front of your face. Most of these subliminal messages come through the television.

Today we have thousands of channels. It would only make sense that there would be thousands of companies who owned and controlled those channels, correct? Yet, this is not the case. The following is a list of the few who control the many.

Disney, National Amusements, Time Warner, Viacom, News Corp, Bertelsmann AG, Sony, General Electric, Vivendi SA and Lagardère Group.

The Telecommunications Act of 1996 was the first major revamping of telecommunications law in nearly 62 years in the United States—supplanting the Communications Act of 1934. This led to a major media consolidation. The Act was approved by the 104th Congress on January 3, 1996 and was signed into law by President Bill Clinton on February 8, 1996. The Act was allegedly intended to promote competition. Instead, it continued the historic industry consolidation that began under the Reagan administration. Those actions reduced the number of major media companies from about fifty in 1983, to only ten in 1996. The ten in 1996 was then reduced to six in 2005. An FCC study found that the Act led to a drastic decline in the number of radio station owners, despite the fact that the actual number of commercial stations in the United States had increased. What this tells you is that they control the information you think is true and real. Consequently they have to saturate the news channels with nothing but murder, rape and terror. How often do you see a good clean story in the news? With this power they are able to produce the Orwellian double-speak doctrine. For example, the War in Iraq is to defend America from weapons of mass destruction. Oops! No weapons? No problem. We fought the war to free the Iraqi people.

Shortly after the 9/11 Terror Attacks, Colin Powell bluntly stated that they had an abundance of evidence to prove that Obama, I mean, Osama Bin Laden was behind the attacks. Colin Powell claimed that everyone would bear witness to the abundance of evidence. From the time of this writing, over 2,500 days have elapsed since Mr. Powell made that statement. Where is the evidence Colin? "We can't disclose information due to national security issues." National Security? I guess they did not view the attack as a breech of national security. But if the security was already breeched, what was the issue?

We do not realize how much of an affect words can have on people. Words are chosen carefully, specifically to change moods or get us to act the way they want us to act. What a coincidence that whenever something happens, every news outlet picks up the same exact phrase and pounds it in your head. All mainstream media outlets are corporate owned and corporate controlled. If anyone within the media corporate structure gets out of line, they will be dealt with.

Within this written documentary, there are many bombshell articles reported by the mainstream media. For the most part, the articles only appear for one or two days and then they are forgotten. But if Britney Spears breaks a nail, it will be on the news for a month! Go figure…

FEDERAL EMERGENCY MANAGEMENT AGENCY (FEMA)

In the United States of America, you have a government agency that does not involve itself in public disclosures. No citizen can accurately estimate its budget. It has the power to suspend laws, move entire populations, arrest and detain people without a warrant, hold them without trial, seize property, food supplies, transportation systems, and can suspend the United States Constitution. Individual rights (the little that we have nowadays) can be suspended. This agency was not created under constitutional law or by the United States Congress. It came into existence by way of Presidential Executive Order 12127. Even the Central Intelligence Agency has to answer to Congress (only in theory). The organization I am speaking about is none other than FEMA. As always, they give the people something the people believe will protect them. They tell you to accept this agency and these new laws because it is for your own good. When FEMA was created, it had one function, and that function was only to assure the continuity of government in the case of a nuclear attack.

Though it may be the most powerful organization in the United States, very few people know its function. FEMA was created in a series of executive orders. A presidential executive order, whether constitutional or not, becomes law by simply getting published in the federal registry. Here are just a few executive orders associated with FEMA that would suspend the Constitution and the Bill of Rights. These executive orders have been on record for nearly thirty years and could be enacted by the stroke of the president's pen.

EXECUTIVE ORDER 10990 allows the government to take over all modes of transportation and control of highways and seaports.

EXECUTIVE ORDER 10995 allows the government to seize and control the communication media.

EXECUTIVE ORDER 10997 allows the government to take over all electrical power, gas, petroleum, fuels and minerals.

EXECUTIVE ORDER 10998 allows the government to take over all food resources and farms.

EXECUTIVE ORDER 11000 allows the government to mobilize civilians into work brigades under government supervision.

EXECUTIVE ORDER 11001 allows the government to take over all health, education and welfare functions.

On July 5, 1987, the Miami Herald published reports on FEMA's new goals. The goal was to suspend the U.S. Constitution in the event of a national crisis. These events include, a nuclear war, violent and widespread internal dissent, or national opposition to a U.S. military invasion abroad. Of course, two years later we had the invasion of Panama, and two years after that, the first invasion of Iraq.

Hurricane Katrina really opened people's eyes (those who were paying attention) to FEMA's real intent on American soil. The Jefferson Parish President, Mr. Aaron Broussard (pictured below), was interviewed on Meet the Press and literally broke down in tears as he spoke the truth about FEMA's criminal acts during the tragedy. "We have been abandoned by our own country. Hurricane Katrina will go down in history as one of the worst storms ever to hit an American coast, but the aftermath of Hurricane Katrina will go down as one of the worst abandonment of Americans on American soil ever in U.S. history," states Broussard.

Aaron Broussard

Meet the Press

He further goes on to say, "We had Wal-Mart deliver three trucks of water, trailer trucks of water. FEMA turned them back. They said we didn't need them. This was a week ago. FEMA, we had 1,000 gallons of diesel fuel on a Coast Guard vessel docked in my parish. The Coast Guard said, 'Come get the fuel right away.' When we got there with our trucks, they got a word; 'FEMA says don't give you the fuel.' Yesterday-yesterday-FEMA comes in and cuts all of our emergency communication lines. They cut them without notice. Our sheriff, Harry Lee, goes back in, he reconnects the line. He posts armed guards on our line and says, 'No one is getting near these lines.'"

It appears Mr. Broussard was reading from a script in the beginning of the interview, perhaps saying what the powers that be wanted him to say. He finally broke down and spilled the truth right on national television. But of course, it was not major news for all the major news outlets. It was brushed under the rug as just another negligent act of government. How is it possible that a government agency interfering in a hurricane relief effort (cutting power lines and turning away water) did not make your 6:00 o'clock or 10:00 o'clock news? For those of you who do not believe in conspiracy theories, you would have called me a liar and a conspiracy nut if I would have told you this story without verification. Are your eyes beginning to open? Are you beginning to suspect that maybe these people are not here to help you? They most certainly were not here to help Mr. Broussard.

Two weeks after his September 4th appearance on meet the press, Mr. Broussard made another appearance—only to be demonized and discredited. There is no question that if he would not have revealed the evil doings of FEMA during Katrina, the powers that be would have left him alone. Instead, the host of "Meet the Press," Tim Russert, quickly tried to make Broussard seem unreliable. Russert pressed Broussard on his account of the tragedy concerning the Parish's emergency services director's mother, who drowned in a nursing home during the hurricane. Although this should have been a side issue, Broussard defended himself by stating that the story of the drowning was related to him by his staff, and he was not inclined to interrogate someone who had just lost their mother.

Tim Russert and other media pundits should have been asking Mr. Broussard about FEMA's criminal activities. But of course, Mr. Broussard's comments with regard to FEMA have not been formally addressed. Several months later, the Jefferson Parish Action Committee (http://www.recallbroussard.com) filed a petition with the Louisiana Secretary of State to remove Mr. Broussard as President of the Jefferson Parish. The committee claims that Broussard was incompetent in his role during Hurricane Katrina, but they make no claims against the criminal activities of FEMA. OUTRAGEOUS!!

Sources: http://www.msnbc.msn.com/id/9438988/
http://www.msnbc.msn.com/id/9219975/

3

SECRET SOCIETIES

Many people try to identify the role secret societies have played in history. Many truth seekers mistakenly paint a brush over freemasonry and then credit freemasonry with all the ills of the world. If you learn anything from this written documentary, learn the fact that the enemy is much more sophisticated than you imagine. They will never be confined to just one group of people.

Alan Axelrod, author of the *International Encyclopedia of Secret Societies and Fraternal Orders*, defines a secret society as possessing three distinct characteristics. He writes that the organization is exclusive, it claims to own special secrets, and it shows a strong inclination to favor its own members. David V. Barrett, the author of *Secret Societies: From the Ancient and Arcane to the Modern and Clandestine*, has a different way to define what does, and does not qualify as a secret society. He interprets a secret society as any group that possesses the following characteristics: (1) Carefully graded and progressed teachings that are (2) available only to selected individuals. (3) These teachings lead to hidden (and 'unique') truths that bring personal benefits beyond the reach, and even the understanding, of the uninitiated. Barrett goes on to write, "A further characteristic common to most secret societies is the practice of rituals which non-members are not permitted to observe or even to know the existence of." Another characteristic secret societies may have is that, in extreme cases, they may be required to take a sworn oath. The sworn oath would be to the effect of concealing or denying their membership in the organization and acknowledging the indicated penalties for not doing so.

To belong, to have status, and to understand certain secret mysteries have always been a key ingredient to attract men of renowned wealth and power. The idea of a special hidden knowledge has existed since the dawn of time. If you were to go back in time, you would learn that the elites of nearly every society have always kept certain knowledge secret and to themselves. Knowledge is kept secret from the masses in order to maintain control over those masses. This is a big part of how the few control the many. For example, today there is knowledge (as there has always been) that there is no real need to use gasoline to run an automobile. The electric car was developed decades ago. However that would empower the people to detach themselves from oil dependency.

There is also evidence of advanced knowledge during ancient times. We see the pyramids in Egypt and South America and wonder how it was done. There is no question that there were two types of ancient people on the planet. Some had advanced technological knowledge, and others were dumb as a rock. The few who wanted to share that knowledge for the good of their people had to do so in secret. These good men (and women) also had to set up secret societies to protect themselves from the ignorant masses that would kill them on the direct or indirect orders of the Unknowns. This is still happening today. People who try to teach the truth are always persecuted and ridiculed by people who have accepted the reality given to them by the Unknowns.

Although no one can pinpoint how old the concepts of secret societies are, one interesting thing to note is that Jesus the Christ also belonged to a secret order.

Hebrews 5:5-6 (King James Version)

5. So also Christ glorified not himself to be made an high priest; but he that said unto him, Thou art my Son, to day have I begotten thee.
6. As he saith also in another place, Thou art a priest for ever after <u>the Order of Melchisedec</u>.

BRITISH-ISRAEL WORLD FEDERATION

Many "truthers" or those associated with what is called "The Truth Movement" rarely speak about a group that was very influential in the scheme of the so-called elites. The group I am referring to is commonly known as the British-Israel World Federation. It is no secret that the British Government played a major roll in creating the State of Israel. Some researchers also teach that the royal British families have a Jewish connection.

The origin of the word "Britain" probably derives from "*Berith*," a Hebrew word for *pact* or *covenant*, and "*ish*" the Hebrew word for "male living being." It symbolizes the pact between God and Abraham. However, the main definition might be derived from the Celtic word, *Pritani*, "painted people/men," in reference to the islands inhabitants' use of body paint and tattoos. What the Unknowns like to do is have two meanings for almost everything. There is one meaning for you (usually false or confusing) and one meaning for them (usually the true etymology).

Before I proceed, I would like to make it clear that the British-Israel World Federation has nothing to do with real Jewish people or their religion. In fact, it is more of a Judeo-Christian group. The early traces of British-Israelism occurred in 1649, when John Sadler published a book entitled, *The Rights of the Kingdom*. In the book, he attempted to trace resemblances between Hebrew and English law. He also attempted to make a resemblance between Hebrew and English customs. The federation would later be founded in London, on July 3, 1919.

The congressional documents found on pages 82 & 83 of this book will give you a better understanding of the role that the British-Israel World Federation group has played in the one world government fraud. Keep in mind that this article was written in 1940 and was being looked at by Congress. It is also very important to note that neither the State of Israel, nor the United Nations was in existence at this time. The League to Enforce the Peace was a primer to get the people ready for the United Nations. I find it interesting that both the State of Israel and the United Nations share the same flag colors.

It is also important to realize that many of the people discussed as the main power players in these documents are members of Skull and Bones. This group (Skull & Bones) was brought to America by President Taft's grandfather, Alphonso Taft, whose grandson (President Taft) helped find the League for the Settlement of International Disputes, which became the League to Enforce the Peace, and then the League of Nations. They always pass their schemes off to the people as something positive, while having a nefarious agenda behind every idea.

If you connect the dots, you will see the hexagram.

The Hexagram

Symbol of the first Jewish Congress

It is important to note that the Roman Catholic Church kept certain ties with the British Royals, even after they split from the church. The Catholic Church was a staunch supporter of Hitler and it influenced South American Catholic countries to open their doors to Nazi war criminals. The church also endorsed Operation Paper Clip. This operation allowed an estimated 1,500 German doctors and scientist to flee to the United States. It is a known fact that Nazi scientists were recruited to work for NASA and Russia's Space Agency.

Operation Paperclip was authorized by President Harry Truman in 1945. However, the order to authorize the operation had a special decree. The decree stated that anyone found to have been a member of the Nazi Party and more than an ostensible participant in its activities, or an active supporter of the Nazi-Party, would be excluded from the operation. The decree did not prevent top Nazi scientist from working for NASA. Top NASA Nazis included Wernher von Braun, Arthur Rudolph, Kurt Debus, and Hubertus Strughold. These demons were cleared to continue their work for the United States. Their war crimes were apparently forgotten and covered up. Justice for Jews who were persecuted at the hands of these demons was not a priority. Instead, the United States and Russia pillaged and ransacked Hitler's regime for the best and brightest Nazis. This is why the United States and Russia led the way in space technology after World War II.

Source: http://www.archives.gov/iwg/declassified-records/rg-330-defense-secretary/

Hitler and his administration have gone down in history as one of the most criminal of all time. And yet, many governments, banks, and corporations had their hands in his stuff. The Catholic Church (which operates as a corporation) was also involved with the Nazis.

When viewed from above, you can clearly see the Vatican courtyard is shaped like a keyhole. You will also notice that within the "keyhole" of the Vatican courtyard, you have two crosses superimposed on each other. This is the same exact symbol found on the British Union Jack flag. *Refer to*: http://jordanmaxwell.com/

On April 20, 1939, Archbishop Orsenigo celebrated Hitler's birthday. The celebrations, which were actually started by Pacelli (Pope Pius XII), became a tradition. Every year on April 20, Cardinal Bertram of Berlin sent a letter which read:

> **"Warmest congratulations to the Fuhrer in the name of the bishops and the dioceses in Germany" and added with "fervent prayers which the Catholics of Germany are sending to heaven on their altars."**

Source: Hitler's Pope: The Secret History of Pius XII, by John Cornwell

British Israelism, Catholicism, and Nazism seemed like one big happy family. If your family got along like this, you would be one happy camper.

In 1933, Hitler and the Pope made an agreement to not get in each others way. This agreement is known as the *Reichskonkordat*. It stated that Hitler and the Reich would not interfere with the Catholic Church, and in return, the Church would not comment on politics and the Reich. The agreement was signed into law on July 20, 1933 by Cardinal Eugenio Pacelli and Franz von Papen on behalf of Pope Pius XI and President Paul von Hindenburg. Although history shows that some Catholic Priests violated the treaty and helped Jews escape persecution, the Church was not harmed by the Reich. As a matter of fact, the *Reichskonkordat* agreement still survives as law in Germany today.

The signing of the Reichskonkordat on July 1933. From Left to Right: German Vice-Chancellor Franz von Papen, representing Germany, Giuseppe Pizzardo, Cardinal Pacelli, Alfredo Cardinal Ottaviani, German ambassador Rudolf Buttman.

Source: The National Catholic Weekly
http://www.americamagazine.org/content/article.cfm?article_id=3131

UNITED STATES · OF AMERICA

Congressional Record

PROCEEDINGS AND DEBATES OF THE 76th CONGRESS, THIRD SESSION

Steps Toward British Union, a World State, and
International Strife—Part I

REMARKS
OF

HON. J. THORKELSON
OF MONTANA

IN THE HOUSE OF REPRESENTATIVES

Had we adhered to the Constitution as it was given to us, we would have been secure and safe today.

Therefore, it is our duty, in the interest of our people and in the interest of this Republic of the United States, to ponder seriously and to give fullest consideration to solving the problem which now confronts the world. In doing so, I am rather inclined to believe that the real American people will decide without hesitation, to return to those fundamental principles that were set forth in the Constitution of the United States. Let no one tell you that this instrument is not

---

PROCEEDINGS AND DEBATES OF THE

Steps Toward British Union, a World State, and International Strife—Part I

REMARKS
OF

HON. J. THORKELSON
OF MONTANA

IN THE HOUSE OF REPRESENTATIVES
Monday, August 19, 1940

Mr. THORKELSON. Mr. Speaker, in order that the American people may have a clearer understanding of those who over a period of years have been undermining this Republic, in order to return it to the British Empire, I have inserted in the RECORD a number of articles to prove this point. These articles are entitled "Steps Toward British Union, a World State, and International Strife." This is part I, and in this I include a hope expressed by Mr. Andrew Carnegie, in his book entitled "Triumphant Democracy." In this he expresses himself in this manner:

Let men say what they will, I say that as surely as the sun in the heavens once shone upon Britain and America united, so surely is it one morning to rise, to shine upon, to greet again the reunited states—the British-American Union.

This statement is clear, and the organizations which Mr.

in close cooperation with world internationalist organizations.

Before 1917, foreign influence came mainly from Anglo-American groups. Since the World War, these groups have been fortified by the international financiers and the internationalists, or the so-called minority group. The pressure is therefore more than double, for combined, these groups control all avenues of communication and are now using them to further their plan of British domination to establish a world federation of states.

Let me call your attention to the fact that on the reverse of the great seal of the United States, which appears on our dollar bills, you will find the exact symbol of the British-Israel world federation movement. This symbol is also carried on literature of other organizations promoting a world government and a world religion. At the bottom of the circle surrounding the pyramid, you will find the wording: "Novus Ordo Seclorum." It was this new order that was advocated by Clinton Roosevelt several hundred years ago; recently in Philip Dru, and now followed by the Executive.

Do you not think, as good American people, that the administration has gone far from constitutional government, when there is inscribed a symbol on the reverse of our great seal, that advocates a new order? Yes, an order which means the destruction of our Republic as formulated in the Constitution of the United States.

It may also interest you to know that this contemplated "Union Now," as advocated by Clarence Streit, will be under the control of Great Britain, and is a movement to return the United States as a colony in the British Empire. Should we become a part of this union, our traditional rights and liberties will be lost, and we will have no greater status than an English possession. This was the dream of Cecil Rhodes and Andrew Carnegie, when the latter wrote his book, Triumphant Democracy, in 1893.

Steps Toward British Union, a World State, and Internal Strife—Part V

This whole document can be found in its' entirety at http://www.taroscopes.com/miscellanous-pages/congrecord.pdf and can be found as posted here at http://www.jordanmaxwell.com/articles/british-israel/index.html

The State of Israel was not formed by Jewish people, nor was it formed for Jewish people. Israel is located in a strategic spot in the Middle East for military purposes and to control trade. Have you ever asked how much oil is in Israel? The answer is zero, *nada*, close to nil. Why then does the United States and Great Britain support Israel with weapons, money, and technology?" Why not support and build up a Middle Eastern country that has an abundance of oil? The answer is simple. They are not there for oil. Gaining control of the oil in the Middle East is only a means to an end. Let us examine some of the things that are done, or not done, to keep using Israel as an aggressor and an oppressor.

1.   The United States awards Israel about $5 billion in aid each year.
2.   Israel is the only country in the Middle East that has nuclear weapons.
3.   Israel is the only country in the Middle East that for years refused to sign the nuclear non-proliferation treaty and barred international inspectors from its sites.
4.   Israel currently occupies territories of two sovereign nations (Lebanon and Syria) in defiance of United Nations Security Council resolutions.
5.   Israeli Foreign Ministry has paid two American public relations firms to promote Israel to Americans.

Israel turns to P.R. firm for makeover amid violence
by Peter Hermann
Baltimore Sun
29 July 2001

JERUSALEM – They have worked with Weight Watchers, the New York Yankees and the Greater Miami Convention & Visitors Bureau. Now the experts at Rubenstein Associates, a public relations company, are taking on a new client: the state of Israel, which hopes to spruce up its image in the deadly conflict with the Palestinians. The New York-based agency, hired this year, has generated several suggestions. First, reduce the number of security guards hovering around Prime Minister Ariel Sharon. The strapping special forces men with dark sunglasses make the hawkish leader look constantly under siege. Next, paint the Israeli military assault rifles that shoot rubber bullets purple or orange – to make it clear to television viewers that soldiers are firing nonlethal rounds. Then, clean up the mess left behind from hours of fighting on both sides: the shooting, shelling, rock throwing and the burning of tires, buses and cars. The idea, the company says, is to "create a sterile and less threatening scene." Government officials said they are taking the recommendations seriously, including the idea of painting the rifles. "This is not a fashion statement," said Emmanuel Nahshon, deputy spokesman for the Ministry of Foreign Affairs. "The idea is to convey to the public that our soldiers are firing rubber bullets, and not live ammunition. It is a daily fight for Israel's image." But Palestinian officials and young boys interviewed at the Ayosh Junction in the West Bank town of Ramallah, one place singled out by Rubenstein as a problem area, say the proposals prove Israel would rather save face than lives. "If they want to look better, they have to stop shooting," said Nabil Abu Rdeineh, a spokesman for Palestinian leader Yasser Arafat. At least 484 Palestinians, 124 Israelis and 13 Israeli Arabs have been killed since the Palestinian uprising began at the end of September. Officials at Rubenstein declined to comment, as did a spokesman for Sharon. Questions were referred to the foreign minister's office and to the Israeli consul general in New York, Alon Pinkas. Pinkas said that the cosmetic changes being recommended are only part of the strategy and that the company first and foremost told the Israelis to quickly release accurate information about daily events. "Good policy will translate into good P.R.," Pinkas said. Members of the public relations company toured the West Bank as part of their four-month study. They were particularly struck by the Ayosh Junction at the edge of Ramallah – a dividing line between areas of Palestinian and Israeli control and a noted flash point of unrest. They noted that the junction "looks in photographs like a battlefield filled with shells of burnt-out cars, boulders and burning tires." The fire-scarred street, which reaches a virtual dead-end at Israeli-controlled territory, also is littered with shrapnel – a convenient backdrop for television news crews based in nearby Jerusalem that need quick video to illustrate the uprising. "It is a war zone," said Pinkas, the consul general. "But there are certain areas that should be cleaned, if not for CNN's sake, then for the welfare of the Jews and the Arabs. But Israel is not going to invade to clean." Crisis management has long been a specialty of the 500-client, 190-employee firm that Howard J. Rubenstein founded in 1954. Miami's Convention & Visitors Bureau hired the firm to help burnish the beaches' image after tourist murders in 1993. Other clients, according to the firm's website, have included New York Yankees owner George Steinbrenner, Yeshiva University, publishing magnate Rupert Murdoch and Sarah, the Duchess of York.

All of this stinks to high heaven, but no one wants to talk about it. The problem is that most people do not know what a conspiracy theory is. Something can only be a theory if it is based on pure belief. For example, the people who believe that 18 or 19 Arabs with box cutters hi-jacked four airplanes on September 11, 2001, are conspiracy theory believers. Ask anyone—who accepts that Arabs with box cutters hi-jacked four American airliners—"Why do you believe that?" The only possible reply must be that it was told to them by none other than their beloved government and lying corporate media. We all know that the government would never lie, right? It is amazing how people who question the official story get tagged with the "conspiracy theorist" label, and those who believe the theory given to them without any evidence or proof get a free pass in the conspiracy conundrum. (The 9/11 Attacks will be covered in more detail with the next volume, "The War on Terror Fraud.")

This type of mentality needs to be destroyed if the common folk want to regain even an inkling of their freedom. I know that regaining that freedom is going to be difficult. How do you free someone who believes that they are already free? The elite know that physical slavery will always fail. Under physical slavery, the slaves knew where they stood and who their enemy was. The slave will always rebel against that type of slavery. But how can you rebel against something that you believe does not exist? The new system they have put in place is very clever. In the New World Order system, the slave must be a willing participant in his own enslavement. A case in point; they make you believe that you own your house, but if you do not pay your property taxes, the real owners will come and take it from you. You also believe that you own your car, but if you do not register it to them, the real owners will take your car by force. If you try to defend your property, they will take it away with violence. They will call upon a person (policeman) who you employ by way of paying taxes. The police have been basically relieved of their duty to protect and serve the people. Now they protect and serve the policy of the state. This is why their name was changed from peace officers to police (policy) officers. They are not interested in what is fair and proper. They are only interested in upholding the policy of the state. This is why they issue parking tickets and traffic tickets with knowledge that there is no injured party. The next time that you get a parking ticket, demand to cross-examine the complaining officer and ask him, "Is there an injured party present in this court room as a result of my parking?" (Refer to volume four: *Slaves by Law*)

These are only small examples of the voluntary slavery that we are participants of today. The people who make the decision to no longer participate in their own enslavement are always portrayed as trouble makers or people who hate the government.

THE ORDER OF THE OWL

The owl is a sacred symbol for the so-called elites. The owl goes back to ancient Greece as the bird of the goddess Athena. It was known for its magical powers. Although the owl is a common hieroglyph in ancient Egyptian writings, the owl does not represent any of the known ancient Egyptian deities (gods). What is not usually associated with an owl is the fact that it can see in the dark. It is a nocturnal creature. To that affect, the owl becomes symbolic of those who can see things that the average person cannot see. The Bohemian Club uses the owl as one of its symbols. Although it has been said that the ancient Canaanite/Moabite god (Molech) represents an owl god, I have never found any supporting evidence to that claim. The name Molech derives from the Hebrew word "*Molech*" or Aramaic "*Melch*" which means, "king" or "ruler." In the Bible, the Book of Genesis 14:18 reads:

Genesis 14:18 (King James Version)

[18]And Melchizedek king of Salem brought forth bread and wine: and he was the priest of the most high God.

In this verse, the Hebrew translation for the compound name Melchizedek is "The (my) priest king." It may also be translated as "The (my) king of righteousness." In Genesis 21:22–34, you have a character by the name of Abimelech. This name simply translates as, "The father king or, the king's father." This implies that the name Molech is only a title—such as "lord" or "master." It may not be the actual name of the god spoken of in the Bible. Even so, the Order of the Owl is very prominent in the United States. Take notice of the following illustration. This picture was taken from high-above the Capitol Building in Washington D.C. It can easily be said that you are looking at the depiction of an owl.

Why is there an owl hidden in the top right hand corner of a U.S. dollar bill? What is the purpose of putting it where no one can see it unless the person is instructed to its whereabouts? If you think it is to help prevent counterfeiting, it would be in-effective and a poor attempt against a legitimate counterfeiting ring. Refer to: www.anti-counterfeitcongress.org

Take a magnifying glass and notice the tiny owl that sits inside the crescent shaped symbol. In most ancient cultures, the crescent was a symbol of fertility. It represented the Babylonian Goddess Ishtar, also known as Inanna (Diana) and Allat. The name Allat is the Arabic feminine of the name Allah. The crescent moon symbol of Islam is a remnant of ancient pagan moon worship. The crescent of Islam represents Ishtar as the female Goddess Allat. Symbolically the owl is sitting in the bosom of the mother-goddess, identical to the sun sitting in the bosom of the crescent moon. Although the symbol was picked up by Moslems, its origins go back to ancient Sumer, where Inanna was also known as "The Lady of the Morning." (Refer to volume 5, *The Creation of God, Religion, and the Old World Order.*)

The U.S. dollar is filled with the signs and symbols of those who have captured the country and rule it from behind the scenes. According to the congressional record posted supra, the Reverse Seal of the United States—as found in the back of the dollar bill—is the exact same symbol of the old British-Israel World Federation movement.

**Reverse Seal of the United States
U.S. Post Office – 216 W. Gowe St.
Kent, Washington, Built in 1939**

Modern symbol of B.I.W.F.

*This is the Logo of the
National Press Club, based
in Washington D.C.*

*They have even put, into the
logo, the Capitol Building in
the background – If you
dispute that the image found
around the capitol building
on the previous page is of an
owl, I would say that it is just
another coinky-dink that
again here you have the owl
and the capitol building in
the background. These are
the people that control all the
news in the United States.*

The following excerpt can be found at
http://npc.press.org/about/history.cfm as of 3/27/08

NPC History

*The National Press Club has been a part of Washington life for nearly
100 years. Through its doors have come all of the Presidents of the
United States since Theodore Roosevelt, as well as kings and queens,
prime ministers, premiers, senators, congressmen, cabinet officials,
ambassadors, scholars, entertainers, business leaders, and athletes. Its*

members have included all of the Presidents of the United States since Warren Harding and most have spoken from the Club's podium.

On March 12, 1908, thirty-two newspapermen met at the Washington Chamber of Commerce to discuss starting a club for journalists. At the meeting they agreed to meet again on March 29, 1908 in the F Street parlor of the Willard Hotel to frame a constitution for the National Press Club.

*******Speaking at the National Press Club to mark his retirement, CBS commentator Eric Sevareid summed up what the National Press Club means to its members when he called it the "sanctum sanctorum of American journalists."

"It's the Westminster Hall, it's Delphi, it's Mecca," said Sevareid, "the <u>Wailing Wall for everybody in this country having anything to do with the news business</u>; the only hallowed place I know of that's absolutely bursting with irreverence."

In this ancient wall statue, the Babylonian moon goddess Ishtar (phonetically similar to "Easter") can be seen alongside two owls. Although there is no concrete evidence, Ishtar may be the same as the Greek concept of the goddess Athena. However, myths about Athena were rewritten often in order to adapt to cultural changes over the multiple eras of ancient Greek traditions. That fact alone makes it very difficult to prove the connection between the two goddesses.

THE MASONIC ORDERS

CRAFT FREEMASONRY

SCOTTISH RITE

YORK RITE

Modern day freemasonry, as we know it today, is traced back to London, England in 1717. It is believed James Anderson set up its constitution. In 1717, Anderson, George Payne, and Theopholips Desaguliers came together to form the first Grand Lodge. It has been said that the lodge was birthed in a tavern. What most researchers do not teach is that the formation of the lodge and the existence of the doctrine are two different things. There is no certainty as to when the doctrine of freemasonry was born. However, it is a well accepted fact that freemasonry had existed in England since at least the mid-1600s, and in Scotland since the Shaw statutes were enacted in 1598-1599.

Today, it is no longer a secret that many of the founding fathers of the United States were Freemasons. Then again, it goes deeper than just the United States. Most of the countries colonized by European powers were involved in freemasonry or other secret societies. For those that try to keep up with what is referred to as "the New World Order," keep in mind that the Americas were referred to as "The New World." This does not imply that all Freemasons had intentions of enslaving humanity.

As mentioned earlier, prominent Freemasons, such as George Washington, had knowledge that an infiltration of the Masonic Order was apparent.

Today, Freemasons have no idea that their organization is only a shell of what it once was. They live their whole lives waiting to get the secrets, and instead, they are no better than those religious people who died waiting for Jesus. Freemasons are in denial of the fact they have been taken over by the Unknowns. The average Freemason does not know anything! They are nothing but believers! No different than a religious person who has no facts—just a bunch of faith and belief! The original or Operative Masons were builders. They built temples and structures. Who in your local lodge can build anything? Are any of them architects? If the answer is no, then my sister-in-law, who is a real architect, is more of a Mason than the fools dressed up like clowns wearing white gloves (just like clowns wear). The average Freemason is no more involved in a conspiracy than a homeless, intoxicated bum lying on the sidewalk. I know that many patriot friends are fooled into pointing the finger at Freemasons and accusing them of being the Unknowns. We need to stop pointing at any one group and believe they are the culprits. I cannot stress this enough.

THE LIGHT IN FREEMASONRY

In the initiation ceremony of the Apprentice, what is happening when the initiate has on the blindfold? At this point, the inquisitive mind is at work. Once the blindfold is taken off, the light is blinding. The chaos begins with the light. In the beginning, God was alone in the universe. God was alone in the dark. Therefore, in the dark there was peace. When God said, "Let there be light," the chaos commenced. The fetus grows in the dark and its peace is disturbed when it enters the light. Most people call it "When the mother gives light." Just the same, you turn off the lights and cuddle into a fetal position when you desire a good nights rest. If someone clicks on the light during your sleep, your peace has been violated and you may wake up, even if the person clicking on the lights did not make a sound.

Christians refer to Jesus as the light (see John 8:12), Moslems refer to Allah as the light (see surah 24:35- *Al Nur)* and Jews refer to Ha'shem as the light. Freemasonry acknowledges both the Bible and the Koran as Holy books. The question becomes, how could Jesus, Allah, Hashem, and angels be the light, and the devil be the bringer or the bearer of light? Did Lucifer create God? Who named the devil Lucifer? Do you know what Lucifer means? Lucifer is a Latin word meaning "light bearer" from the word *lux, lucis,* meaning "light" and *"ferre"* which means "to bear, bring." It is also a Roman astrological term for "the Morning Star," which refers to the planet Venus. The word used in Hebrew is "Helel ben Shahar" meaning; son of the dawn. Now, go ask a Moslem. Who are you praying to when you make the Subh or Fajr (Dawn) prayer? Are they praying to Allah, or the Son of the Morning?

At-Tariq, "The Night Comer", is the 86th surah (chapter) in the Koran. It begins:

Bismillah ir-Rahman ir-Rahim
1. By the heaven and the Morning Star
2. Ah, what will tell thee what the Morning Star is!
3. The piercing Star!
4. No human soul but hath a guardian over it

Isaiah 14:12 (New King James Version)

"How you are fallen from heaven,
O Lucifer, son of the morning!
How you are cut down to the ground,
You who weakened the nations!

Lucifer has been acknowledged by the Satanic Bible as one of the four crown princes of hell, particularly of the East (who are the Moslems and Jews praying to when they face the east?). Other attributes given to Lucy are Lord of the Air, Bringer of Light, the Morningstar, Intellectualism, and Enlightenment. In science, you have luciferin and luciferase. They are two substances involved in the chemical production of light.

Luciferins- are a class of light-emitting biological pigments that are found in organisms capable of bioluminescence.

Luciferase- is a generic term for enzymes mostly used in nature for bioluminescence. The most common is firefly luciferase (EC 1.13.12.7) which is from the firefly *Photinus pyralis*.

I do not mean to bore you with science. I want you to understand; it is not just symbolism to say that a biological entity (Lucifer) gives off light or is of the light.

A successful way the Unknowns keep certain knowledge secret is to reveal an apparent leaking of it with another secret of their own—a false one. Often, it would contain 10% truth and 90% lies, although sometimes vice versa. I will end this segment by simply stating that believing that the Freemasons are the main conspirators against humanity is inaccurate. Has there been (in history) high-ranking Freemasons who have sold the people out? That is not disputable. However, to say it is "The Masons" would be inaccurate. The fools who follow that idea are off the trail of the real culprits.

THE ORDER OF SKULL & BONES (The Brotherhood of Death)

The Order of Skull and Bones, also known as "The Brotherhood of Death," is a secret society based at Yale University in New Haven, Connecticut. The order was formed in 1832 and the society's alumni organization, which owns its properties and oversees all the organization's activity, is known as the Russell Trust Association. It is named after one of the societies' co-founding members, William Huntington Russell (12 August 1809 – 19 May 1885). Russell was a blue blood descendant of the most noted New England families, such as the Pierpont family, the Hooker, Bingham, and Willet family. William Russell was the first cousin of Samuel Russell. Samuel Russell was the richest opium dealer in the world at the time. Warren Delano, Jr., the grandfather of Franklin Roosevelt (32nd President of the United States and 33rd Degree Freemason) served as the head of Samuel Russell's company, called Operations of Russell and Company in Canton. Both of these men had business ties with John Murray Forbes, the great-granduncle of 2004 presidential candidate and fellow Skull and Bones member, John (Forbes) Kerry. John Murray Forbes' brother, Captain Robert Bennet Forbes (September 18, 1804–November 23, 1889), gained much of his wealth from the opium and China trade. He played a prominent role in the start of the Opium War.

If you are not familiar with the Opium Wars, it was a war between China and Britain concerning the fact that the Chinese Government wanted to put an end to the smuggling of Opium into their country. The British, who were smuggling in the opium from their territories in India, resisted. After China lost the war, Britain forced the Chinese Government to sign the Treaty of Nanking and the Treaty of Tianjin, also known as the Unequal Treaties. These treaties included provisions for the opening of additional ports to foreign trade, allowing the British to freely bring in the opium. By the mid-1830s, the opium trade had become the biggest business in the world. It was greater than any single commodity found anywhere on the planet. It is no coincidence that ever since the Taliban was toppled in Afghanistan, the opium fields have been reactivated to all time highs. Prior to the invasion of Afghanistan, the opium fields were almost eliminated.

Refer to http://opioids.com/afghanistan/index.html.

The Bush administration and others have misled people into believing that the Taliban are the real pushers of opium. With the help of the press and the unsuspecting public, they have accused the Taliban of using the sale of opium as a source of revenue. The reality of the matter is that the so-called British Government (and American Government) is still trafficking opium. The Taliban is just a front for their operation. The blame goes to the Taliban, but the profits go in their pockets. The remaining so-called Taliban forces work for them! This is why they continue to help the so-called Taliban and al-Qaeda forces escape and fly to safety. Shortly after the Afghan War was declared won, the United Islamic Front for the Salvation of Afghanistan (UIF, Jabha-yi Muttahid-i Islami-yi Milli bara-yi Nijat-i Afghanistan), also known as the Northern Alliance, reported that Taliban soldiers were airlifted to Pakistan by U.S. military forces. The Northern Alliance was set up in 1996 to fight against the Taliban. They joined U.S. forces in the war against the Taliban and the search for Bin Laden. In addition, for those who do not know, Pakistan was a financial and military supporter of the Taliban against the Northern Alliance. Do you see the game? The Taliban supports Pakistan (and vice versa) who is supported by the United States. Hence, Taliban and Pakistani forces are flown to safety by the United States.

guardian.co.uk

US helped Taliban to safety, magazine claims

- Oliver Burkeman in New York
- The Guardian,
- Monday January 21, 2002

An American-approved evacuation of Pakistani military officials from the besieged Afghan city of Kunduz last November "slipped out of control", allowing al-Qaida fighters to join the exodus, it was claimed yesterday. "Dirt got through the screen," a US intelligence official told New Yorker magazine. According to the magazine, the US allowed Pakistan's military officials to be flown to safety to preserve the political standing of General Pervez Musharraf, whose survival is seen as crucial to the American war effort.

The exodus - which the administration insisted at the time had not taken place - was intended only to rescue Pakistani officials from Kunduz, which was surrounded by Northern Alliance troops backed by American forces.

But the New Yorker's defence correspondent, Seymour Hersh, quotes a senior intelligence source as saying that Taliban and al-Qaida fighters

slipped on board. "Everyone brought their friends with them," a
defence adviser told him.

The US military may even have directly co-operated in the airlifts,
according to the article, which is based on conversations with
intelligence officials and senior military officers. Two such sources told
Hersh that the US central command was ordered to establish a special
air corridor to guarantee that the rescue flights could proceed safely.
"Unhappy is not the word," said an analyst who worked with Delta
Force, the commando unit charged with destroying Taliban bases on
the ground, describing the army's reaction to the order.

This article can be read in it's entirety at:
http://www.guardian.co.uk/world/2002/jan/21/afghanistan.usa
Also refer to
http://www.newyorker.com/archive/2002/01/28/020128fa_FACT

In the June of 2008, more alleged Taliban and al-Qaeda
forces were broken out of jail in what was referred to as a
"daring jailbreak." This is reminiscent of the British intelligence
officers who were caught dressed as Arabs with fake beards
shooting at Iraqi police. They were arrested, only to be broken
out of jail by British forces. Most of the so-called "insurgency"
in Iraq is being done by the so-called coalition forces—with the
help of their al-Qaeda and Taliban goons.

As stated supra, there was another jailbreak in which
more Taliban and al-Qaeda soldiers escaped. This, of course, led
to more violence in Afghanistan. This translates to mean that
U.S. military presence and coalition forces will be needed for a
while longer, as the fight against the Taliban has been basically
reset. This also means that the Taliban can continue to assist
American and British intelligence agencies (who are the real
drug dealers) in the opium trade.

Sources:
http://www.cnn.com/2008/WORLD/asiapcf/06/14/afghanistan.taliban/
http://xiaodongpeople.blogspot.com/2005/09/british-forces-break-
soldiers-out-of.html
http://www.timesonline.co.uk/tol/news/world/iraq/article568439.ece
http://www.msnbc.msn.com/id/9400104/

A trusted source of news
and information since 1942

By VOA Afghanistan Service
Nangahar Province, Afghanistan
27 May 2008

Afghanistan supplies virtually all of the world's illegal opium. Last year, the country's drug trade was a $4 billion business, <u>half of which alone was produced in the south where the fighting against the Taliban insurgency is the fiercest.</u>
Getting Afghanistan to rid itself of poppy is a pillar of U.S. policy there, because the Taliban use profits from opium as a source of revenue. For Afghans themselves, however, feelings about poppy are conflicted: It's harmful to their country and to their people, but it is also a livelihood for many where instability offers few alternatives.
In the third of a four part series, VOA's Afghan service examines the drug trade in Afghanistan's Nangahar province. VOA's Siri Nyrop narrates.

This article can be read in full at
http://www.voanews.com/english/2008-05-27-voa38.cfm

This article is astonishing, considering the fact that in February of 2001, U.N. drug control officers said that the Taliban's religious militia had nearly wiped out all of the opium production in Afghanistan. Another interesting thing about that article is the fact that the drugs are being developed in the south, where the so-called insurgency is the fiercest. Does this make sense? Aren't the Taliban drug dealers afraid that all the chaos around their drug operation will ruin their gig? Who are the real drug dealers? As you shall read later, the CIA is a major player in the drug business. They are responsible for shipping the drugs into the United States. You can go ahead and connect the dots between the CIA, Skull and Bones and the drug trade.

On October 22, 1945, Secretary of War, Robert P. Patterson (once president of the Council on Foreign Relations), created the Lovett Committee. This committee was chaired by a member of Skull and Bones named Robert A. Lovett. Mr. Lovett was to head up a new arm of U.S. intelligence. This resulted in the creation of the CIA. Many members of Skull and Bones have occupied high positions in the U.S. intelligence communities. The most notable Bonesman would be George Bush Sr., who served as the head of the CIA during the mid 1970s.

Skull and Bones is a very powerful elite secret society in America. This group is very influential and has a substantial grip on American politics. Case in point, out of a population of 300 million people in the United States, the two candidates for the 2004 presidential election, Bush and Kerry, were both members of Skull and Bones. It seems that no matter who we vote for every four years, the elite win, we lose.

washingtonpost.com

Bush, Kerry Share Tippy-Top Secret
Yalies Bush and Kerry Share a Patrician Past Of Skull and Bones

By Don Oldenburg
Washington Post Staff Writer
Sunday, April 4, 2004; Page D01

(in part...) It's no secret that Bush and Kerry are both Yalies. Bush graduated in 1968, Kerry in '66. It's no secret either that they both come from privileged preppy backgrounds. What remains shrouded in mystery is their membership in Skull and Bones, an elite, covert club for which involvement continues long past the last refrain of "Pomp and Circumstance" on graduation day.

Never before have two Bonesmen run against each other for the presidency. It's a coincidence of historic political proportions.

"What is so staggering about two Bonesmen running against each other for president is that it's a tiny club with 15 members a year and only 600-some living at any time. What are the odds?" says Alexandra

Robbins, author of the 2002 book "Secrets of the Tomb: Skull and Bones, the Ivy League, and the Hidden Paths of Power."

Don't bother asking Bush and Kerry the odds. Both would rather advocate raising taxes. Neither talks publicly about Skull and Bones -- except to say he can't talk about it.

Neither man responded to repeated requests for interviews for this article. But when Tim Russert asked Bush about Skull and Bones in February on "Meet the Press," the president said: "It's so secret we can't talk about it." When Russert asked Kerry last August what it meant that both he and Bush are Bonesmen, the Massachusetts senator replied: "Not much because it's a secret."

But the fact that both presidential candidates are Bonesmen raises a different question: How has Skull and Bones imprinted them?

Some critics say Bones produces elitist leaders who are myopic on America's social and economic challenges. Others argue that for presidential candidates to profess loyalty to a secret society -- particularly one that for a time didn't admit minorities and women -- is contrary to democratic principles.

Chicago writer and educator Steve Sewall, son of revered Yale English professor Richard B. Sewall, has even called for Bush and Kerry to resign from Skull and Bones. "They can be loyal to it, but they can't place that loyalty above the loyalty to the nation they serve," he argues.

(continued.....) Skull and Bones was created in 1832 by Yale student William H. Russell, heir to a fortune made in the opium trade. During his travels, Russell linked up with an occult society in Germany and returned to New Haven with thoughts of starting a chapter, according to documents purloined during an 1876 Tomb break-in.

(continued...) A roster of Bones alumni, known as "patriarchs," surfaced in the mid-1980s. Included are names of the nation's oldest, wealthiest and most powerful dynasties -- Whitney, Adams, Lord, Rockefeller, Payne, Pillsbury, Weyerhaeuser. Other famous names on the list: poet Archibald MacLeish; writer John Hersey; political commentator William F. Buckley; Time-Life founder Henry Luce; investment banker Dean Witter Jr. and Morgan Stanley founder Harold

Stanley, among others who built Wall Street; diplomat Averill Harriman and FedEx founder Frederick Smith.

Bush's father, former president George H.W. Bush, is a Bonesman, as was his grandfather, Sen. Prescott Bush. And the family married into even more Bones links on the Walker side. As for Kerry, his brother-in-law from his first marriage was Bones; his wife, Teresa Heinz Kerry, was married to the late Sen. John Heinz, whose father was Bones.

Bones alumni show up as luminaries of the political power grid throughout history -- Supreme Court justices, federal judges, U.S. senators and congressmen, Cabinet members, CIA officials. And, yes, presidents -- though more Bonesmen had the president's ear than the job.

This article can be read in it's entirety at
http://www.washingtonpost.com/ac2/wp-dyn/A48358-2004Apr3?language=printer

The fact that only 15 members get tapped every year, as well as the fact that there is usually well under a thousand Bonesmen alive at any one-time, goes beyond understanding. How does a small minority of people continually occupy positions of authority (power)? Is that not a conspiracy?

Do not worry your pretty little head. Just keep doing what you are doing and the elite will continue to do what they are doing. Who cares if you are a slave that thinks he is free. To the ignorant, the important thing is believing that they are free.

THE COUNCIL ON FOREIGN RELATIONS

The Council on Foreign Relations, which is commonly referred to as "The CFR," is a nonpartisan foreign policy membership organization that was founded in 1921. It is primarily housed at 58 East 68th Street in New York City, although they also have an office in the nation's capital. This is indeed the most influential private organization on American foreign policy.

Members of this council include ex-presidents, ambassadors, secretaries of state, Wall Street investors, international bankers, foundation executives, think tank executives, lobbyist lawyers, NATO and Pentagon military leaders, wealthy industrialists, journalists, media owners and executives, university presidents and key professors, select congressmen, Supreme Court Justices, federal judges, wealthy entrepreneurs, and as many as ten 9/11 Commission members.

In a 1979 memoir written by Arizona Senator Barry Goldwater, he reveals the following:

> *"When a new President comes on board, there is a great turnover in personnel but no change in policy. Example: During the Nixon years Henry Kissinger, CFR member and Nelson Rockefeller's protégé, was in charge of foreign policy. When Jimmy Carter was elected, Kissinger was replaced by Zbigniew Brzezinski, CFR member and David Rockefeller's protégé."*

Since at least the 1960s, every presidential cabinet has been painted with a host of CFR members. Although Ronald Reagan defeated CFR members in both 1980 (Jimmy Carter) and 1984 (Walter Mondale), his cabinet was also a wash with CFR members. The most notable was, of course, big daddy Bush. Perhaps not strange enough, daddy Bush had a connection to John Hinckley. John Hinckley was the character charged with trying to assassinate President Reagan. John Hinckley's father was the chairman of an oil company named Vanderbilt Energy Corp. This company was a significant contributor to big daddy Bush's 1980 Republican presidential primary bid against Ronald Reagan. John Hinckley's brother, Scott Hinckley, was reported to have had a dinner appointment with Neil Bush, the son of daddy Bush and brother of 43rd president George W. Bush, at around the time of the shooting.

It is remarkable as to how the Bush family is constantly involved in suspicious behavior and is never investigated. The poor excuse of an investigation concerning the shooting did not bother to ask serious questions about the relationship between the Bush's and the Hinckley's.

Sources: *The Houston Post*, March 31, 1981 "BUSH'S SON WAS TO DINE WITH SUSPECT'S BROTHER, by Arthur Wiese and Margarte Downing."

President Reagan waves to the crowd moments before shooting

Reagan actually supported Senator Barry Goldwater's 1964 presidential candidacy. During Reagan's own 1980 presidential campaign, he was advocating a limited government and economic *laissez-faire* type of philosophy in a similar manor that Senator Goldwater did. These principals go against the ideals and goals of the CFR. This group has their slimy paws in almost every facet of American life. Here is a list of some current CFR board directors:

- **Board of Directors**

Robert E. Rubin

Co-Chairman; Director and Chairman of the Executive Committee, Citigroup, Inc.

Richard N. Haass
President, Council on Foreign Relations

Fouad Ajami
M. Khadduri Prof. of Middle Eastern Studies, Paul H. Nitze School of

Advanced International Studies, Johns Hopkins University

Madeleine K. Albright
Principal, The Albright Group LLC

Henry S. Bienen

President, Northwestern University

Tom Brokaw

NBC News

Sylvia Mathews Burwell
President, Global Development Program, Bill & Melinda Gates Foundation

Martin S. Feldstein

President, National Bureau of Economic Research

Jami Miscik
Managing Director, Global Head of Sovereign Risk, Lehman Brothers

James W. Owens
Chairman & CEO, Caterpillar Inc.

Colin L. Powell
United States Army (Ret.)

David M. Rubenstein

Co-Founder and Managing Director, The Carlyle Group

Anne-Marie Slaughter
Dean, Woodrow Wilson School of Public and International Affairs, Princeton

University

Joan E. Spero
President, Doris Duke Charitable Foundation

Christine Todd Whitman
President, The Whitman Strategy Group

Fareed Zakaria
Editor, Newsweek International

Source: http://www.cfr.org/about/people/board_of_directors.html

Even with all the notable names that are or have been members over the past 50 years, the CFR is hardly known by the average person. They are rarely mentioned in the mainstream media. This is quite strange, considering the fact that not all of their meetings are private or secret. How can the established media not report on a group that is comprised of the biggest names in business and politics? Do Americans have the right to know exactly who is heading up their foreign policies? Let us examine this.

-In the 1984 presidential race, Walter Mondale was a CFR member. Although Reagan was not, his vice president, daddy Bush, was a member.

-In the 1988 race, both Bush and Michael Dukakis were members of the CFR.

-The 1992 campaign again featured two members, featuring big daddy Bush and Bill Clinton.

-In 1996 Bill Clinton was challenged by fellow CFR member Bob Dole.

-The unforgettable 2000 presidential race had Al Gore, who was a member, and baby Bush, who was not a member, but was close to CFR action by way of his daddy and running mate, Dick Cheney, who was also a member. Again I ask; why doesn't the mainstream media talk about an organization whose members continually appear in positions of power? Why must the common folk be kept ignorant of the Council on Foreign Relations?

THE ILLUMINATI

The very word "Illuminati" is almost always associated with the term "conspiracy theory." However, contrary to popular belief, the Illuminati were, and are, as real as any secret society that survives today. You can research this group in most encyclopedias. This secret society is said to have been founded on May 1, 1776, in Ingolstadt, Bavaria by a Jesuit named Adam Weishaupt. It is no coincidence that the Illuminati immerged during the Age of Enlightenment. The word "Illuminati" comes from the word "Illumine," meaning to light up or to be of the light. The original name the group gave themselves was the Perfectibilists. It was not until they infiltrated the lodges of freemasonry that they took hold of the name "Illuminated Ones." Freemasons were already known as the Sons of the Light. Other names attributed to the Perfectibilists are the Bavarian Illuminati and the Illuminati Order. In 1784 Karl Theodor, the Ruler of Bavaria, banned all secret societies in his country. The ban forced the secret societies to become extremely secret—going further underground.

By the time the order was legally banned, it had managed to influence high ranking officials in the Bavarian Government and other governments of Europe. One such official was a diplomat by the name of Xavier von Zwack. Von Zwack is thought to have been a high ranking official in the order. He was the man in possession of the order's documents when his home was searched by authorities.

Although some historians teach that no reliable evidence can be found to support Weishaupt's group survived into the nineteenth century, there is no evidence to suggest the group dissipated into the pages of history. In 1798, a Scottish professor of philosophy at the University of Edinburgh, named James Robison, wrote a book entitled; *The Illuminati; Proofs of a Conspiracy*. In 1783, he had become General Secretary of the Royal Society of Edinburgh. In 1797, Robison's articles for the *Encyclopaedia Britannica* gave an account of the scientific, mathematical, and technological knowledge of that day. It was Robison and a French priest by the name of Abbé Barruel, who independently came to the same conclusions. They concluded that the *Illuminati* had infiltrated European Continental free-masonry. They believed the infiltration led to the events of the French Revolution. Then, it was in 1798, that a reverend by the name of G. W. Snyder sent Robison's book to President George Washington. Reverend Snyder wanted President Washington's opinion on the infiltration of the freemasonic lodges by the Illuminati. As documented earlier, George Washington was certain that the infiltration of some lodges in the United States had taken place.

The eighteenth century, also known as the Age of Enlightenment, has shaped the modern world as we see it today. Whether you believe the Illuminati survived or not is irrelevant. The fact of the matter is that their goals have been accomplished. The monarchs of Europe have been overthrown, an elite few have control of the banking system, the media, and the educational structure. All these goals were documented by the early doctrines of the Illuminati. Does it matter what names they are using today? Who cares if they are called the Twinkie Dinky club? This is the reason why we refer to those at the top of the pyramid as the Unknowns.

Further history of the Illuminati Order reveals that when Xavier von Zwack had his house in Landshut illegally searched by the police, his personal documents and papers were seized. As a result, von Zwack was immediately fired from his government position. Several books, documents, papers, and letters were found during the raid—including over 200 letters written between Weishaupt and the members of the order. The letters dealt with matters of the highest secrecy. The following year after the raid, more documents were confiscated from the houses of Baron Bassus and Count Massenhausen. Among the confiscated documents were tables containing their secret codes, symbols, secret calendar, geographical locations, insignias, ceremonies of initiation, recruiting instructions, statutes, a partial list of members, and about 130 official seals from the government. Apparently, these seals were being used to counterfeit state documents.

All of the seized documents shed light on the Illuminati Order and the danger that was first realized by the Bavarian Government. The Illuminati revelation had become a national emergency. In 1786, the Bavarian Government gathered all of the confiscated documents and made them public in a book entitled, *Original Writings of the Order and Sect of the Illuminati*. This book was circulated to every government and monarch head of Europe in order to warn them of the impending danger. However, just like it happens today, these revelations did very little to alert the public at large. The old adage of a conspiracy being too unbelievable to take serious reared its ugly head.

In an article on eighteenth century Italy, the Encyclopedia Britannica refers to Illuminati cells as "Republican freethinkers." The order was referred to as a "Rationalistic secret society" in an article on Roman Catholicism.

Although the warnings of Professor Robison and Abbé Barruel fell on deaf ears, those deaf ears received no help from Illuminati apologists. In the London *Monthly Magazine* for January 1798, there appeared a letter from Karl August Böttiger. The letter was a reply to Robison's work against the Illuminati. Karl August Böttiger (1760 – 1835) was a German archaeologist, classicist, and a prominent member of the literary and artistic circles in the cities of Weimer and Jena. In his article for the London Monthly Magazine, he charges Robison with making false statements. Böttiger was declaring that the Illuminati Order ceased to exist after 1790. But those who still follow this theory of disappearance are always short of answers. They could never explain how it is possible that the Illuminati's doctrines and goals, as exposed by Robison and Barruel, were accomplished or are in the process of being accomplished—even after the group was supposedly banished and never to be heard from again.

Accomplished goals of the Illuminati

1. Remove the Monarch's of Europe from power.
2. Abolish ownership of private property.
3. Destroy religion (old world order).
4. Separate people from their governments (destroy patriotism).
5. Create a one world government. (United Nations, World Court, International law).

Sources: The Catholic Encyclopedia entry on Illuminati
http://www.newadvent.org/cathen/07661b.htm
http://www.cesnur.org/2005/mi_illuminati_en.htm
Encyclopaedia Britannica, 15th edition. Vol. 22, p. 223, 2b.
Encyclopaedia Britannica, 15th edition. Vol. 26, p. 937, 2b.

4

POWER PLAYERS

It may be easier to find a needle in a hay stack, than it is to clearly define what constitutes power in the pyramid of the elites. Truth seekers can spend hour after hour writing books and lecturing in documentaries about who has real clout and who does not. The information about certain families and corporations that you are about to read will only examine how the power of the Unknowns manifests itself in the world. The reality is that there are those who are only puppets. In most cases, they cannot see the layers of power above them. Nevertheless, there are others who wield more power than their public positions suggest. Baby Bush is a perfect example of the earlier. Anyone can see that baby Bush does not make any decisions. During his entire time in the White House, baby Bush has done nothing but sign things. Whoever believes that baby Bush has more than two working brain cells in his head is not the sharpest nail in the box.

THE BUSH FAMILY

Although most of the public is unaware, baby Bush's grandfather, Prescott Bush, directed a bank that helped finance Hitler's Nazi Machine. It is amazing that this was not an issue during any of baby Bush's presidential campaigns. How is it that a story like this did not hit all the major networks and all the major newspapers?

The following article was obtained from fox.com and can be found at http://www.foxnews.com/story/0,2933,100474,00.html as of 4/1/08

DOCUMENTS: BUSH'S GRANDFATHER DIRECTED BANK TIED TO MAN WHO FUNDED HITLER

Friday, October 17, 2003

WASHINGTON — *President Bush's grandfather was a director of a bank seized by the federal government because of its ties to a German industrialist who helped bankroll Adolf Hitler's rise to power, government documents show.*

Prescott Bush was one of seven directors of Union Banking Corp., a New York investment bank owned by a bank controlled by the Thyssen family, according to recently declassified National Archives documents reviewed by The Associated Press. Fritz Thyssen was an early financial supporter of Hitler, whose Nazi party Thyssen believed was preferable to communism. The documents do not show any evidence Bush directly aided that effort. His position with Union Banking never was a political issue for Bush, who was elected to the Senate from Connecticut in 1952. Reports of Bush's involvement with the seized bank have been circulating on the Internet for years and have been reported by some mainstream media. The newly declassified documents provide additional details about the Union Banking-Thyssen connection. Trent Duffy, a spokesman for President Bush, declined to comment.

Union Banking was owned by a Dutch bank, Bank voor Handel en Scheepvaardt N.V., which was "closely affiliated" with the German conglomerate United Steel Works, according to an Oct. 5, 1942, report from the federal Office of Alien Property Custodian. The Dutch bank and the steel firm were part of the business and financial empire of Thyssen and his brother, Heinrich Thyssen-Bornemisza, the report said. The 4,000 Union Banking shares owned by the Dutch bank were registered in the names of the seven U.S. directors, according a document signed by Homer Jones, chief of the division of investigation and research of the Office of Alien Property Custodian, a World War II-era agency that no longer exists. E. Roland Harriman, the bank chairman and brother of former New York Gov. W. Averell Harriman, held 3,991 shares. Bush had one share.

Both Harrimans and Bush were partners in the New York investment firm of Brown Brothers, Harriman and Co., which handled the financial transactions of the bank as well as other financial dealings with several other companies linked to Bank voor Handel that were confiscated by the U.S. government during World War II. Union Banking was seized by the government in October 1942 under the Trading with the Enemy Act. No charges were brought against Union Banking's American directors. The federal government was too busy trying to fight the war, said Donald Goldstein, a professor of public and international affairs at the University of Pittsburgh.

"We did not have the resources to do these things," Goldstein said. Fritz Thyssen broke with the Nazis in 1938 over their persecution of Catholics and Jews, and fled to Switzerland. He later was arrested and spent 1941 to 1945 in a Nazi prison. His brother lived in Switzerland from 1932 to 1947 but continued to operate businesses in Germany. The new documents were first reported by freelance writer John Buchanan in The New Hampshire Gazette.

Also refer to; *http://coat.ncf.ca/our_magazine/links/54/54_22-23.pdf*
http://www.nhgazette.com/the-bushnazi-stories/bushnazi-link-confirmed/

The Bush family has kept mostly silent about this issue, although some Bush sympathizers have made the claim that Prescott Bush had no idea his bank was funding the Nazis. This claim is highly unlikely, due to the fact that Prescott Bush founded the bank along with a fellow by the name of Cornelis Lievense. Lievense served as the president of the bank while Prescott Bush was the vice-president. Cornelis Lievense was a Dutch businessman with vast wealth. He spearheaded several corporations during his business career. One such company was the Domestic Fuel Corporation, which was blacklisted by the Canadian Government in 1940 for the same reasons his bank with Prescott Bush was seized in the United States. Are we to really believe that Prescott Bush had no idea Cornelis Lievense was doing business with the Nazis? You also have E. Roland Harriman, who was the brother and business partner of W. Averell Harriman. It is an undisputable historical fact that the Harrimans had been doing business with Hitler's regime.

In 1942, many of the Harriman's business interests where seized by the United States Government under the Trading with the Enemy Act. Among the companies seized were Holland-American Trading Corporation, The Seamless Steel Equipment Corporation, Silesian-American Corporation, and of course, the Union Banking Corporation. It is also a well accepted fact that E. Roland Harriman was a close personal friend of Prescott Bush. They were both Yale graduates and members of the secretive Skull and Bones fraternity. Again, the theory that Prescott Bush was not aware of these Nazi ties does not hold water.

Sources:
http://www.guardian.co.uk/world/2004/sep/25/usa.secondworldwar
"Canada Blacklists Two U.S. Concerns", *New York Times*, Mar 28, 1940, p. 44

The Bush family is one of those bottom feeding families of the so-called elite who have worked their way up the ranks because of their bloodline and ruthlessness. It is no coincidence that grandpa Bush had ties with the Nazis. The United States, as well as most western countries, has adopted the type of fascist ideals that were first visited by Hitler. I am not indicating Hitler is the father of fascism. I am simply stating that his model of fascism is what has been implemented by the cronies of the Unknowns. But then again, it can be argued that Hitler was nothing but another creation of the Unknowns to further their agenda. Hitler's mistreatment of the Jews was the pretext for setting up the STATE of ISRAEL. The Zionist had the sympathy of the world on their side. This enabled the goals of the Jewish Congress of 1897 and the Balfour Declaration of 1917 to come into fruition.

The Balfour Declaration was a letter from the British Foreign Secretary, Arthur James Balfour, to Second Baron, Lord Walter Rothschild. The letter basically stated that the British Government was in great favor of a Jewish State in Palestine. European powers have been in place there ever since the decline of the imperial monarchy of the Ottoman Empire.

The Treaty of Lausanne put an official end to Ottoman rule on July 24, 1923. The Ottoman Empire was reduced into what is now called the Republic of Turkey, which was officially recognized on October 29, 1923. After the decline of the Ottoman Empire, the taking of Palestine was a cake walk. In 1916, after the eminent decline and eventual down fall of the Ottoman Empire, France and Britain came together under the *Sykes-Picot* agreement to determine what parts of the old Empire they would carve up for themselves. Certainly this could have been in the cards even before the fall of the Ottomans. With the Ottomans out of the way, the British could expand their powers beyond the Arabian Peninsula. In fact, it was the British who influenced and encouraged the Arab states to revolt against the Ottoman Empire. In November of 1918, the Anglo-French Declaration stated Great Britain and France would; *"assist in the establishment of indigenous Governments and administrations in Syria and Mesopotamia by setting up national governments and administrations deriving their authority from the free exercise of the initiative and choice of the indigenous populations."* Unfortunately for the Jewish Congress, the *Sykes-Picot Agreement* was made public by the Bolsheviks immediately after the Bolshevik Revolution. The Bolshevik revelation took place three weeks after the Balfour Declaration was written.

Only a year after the Balfour Declaration was written, the indigenous Arabs sensed the European powers, who had helped them defeat the Ottoman Empire, would soon replace the Ottomans as their new masters. In a parade conducted by the Zionists to celebrate the one year anniversary of the Balfour Declaration, a group of Arab Muslims and Arab Christians came together to protest the carrying of what is now known as the flag of Israel. Members of the British Government became weary of the excessive support their country was giving the Zionist. With public support reaching low levels on this matter, Winston Churchill sent a letter to the British Commissioner of Palestine, Herbert Samuel, stating the following:

> *In both Houses of Parliament there is growing movement of hostility, against Zionist policy in Palestine, which will be stimulated by recent Northcliffe articles. I do not attach undue importance to this movement, but it is increasingly difficult to meet the argument that it is unfair to ask the British taxpayer, already overwhelmed with taxation, to bear the cost of imposing on Palestine an unpopular policy.*

Despite the letter, after World War II Churchill played his part in setting up the State of Israel.

Britain and Palestine, 1921–1924   57

outset. As early as March 1920, when Palestine was still under Foreign Office control, a minute by Hubert Young demonstrated that the possibility of 'abandoning' the government's pro-Zionist policy was a recurring theme in official circles.[55] Domestic opposition to Britain's policy in Palestine focused on two main themes: its tax implications, and the promises made by Britain (as represented by Sir Henry McMahon) to the Arabs (as represented by Sharif Hussein of Mecca) in the famed 1915 correspondence. These promises were argued to be in direct contradiction to the Balfour pledge made two years later.

It was the potential tax burden that was the earlier focus of public scrutiny, being taken up by the press within months of the July 1920 establishment of the civil administration in Palestine. On 5 February 1921, for example, the *Daily Express* wrote that the terms of the mandate made clear the extent of the financial burden at a time when the British people were already 'crushed by taxation, oppressed by restricted trade and widespread unemployment', and that there was no reason why Britain should squander resources in the 'arid wastes of the Middle East'.[56] Despite the March 1921 conference convened by Churchill in Cairo which aimed to reduce imperial expenditure in the Middle East,[57] the press continued on this theme. The *Times*, which initially had supported the Balfour Declaration, by 1922 was raising the question of whether Britain could afford to implement it.[58] Lord Northcliffe, the proprietor of the *Times* and the *Daily Mail*, visiting Palestine in early 1922, observed that Palestine Zionists 'seemed inclined altogether to overestimate the amount of interest taken by the British public in Zionism'.[59]

Sources: http://www.totallyjewish.com/news/national/c-7480/90th-anniversary-of-balfour-declaration/
Sahar Huneidi, Walid Khalidi A Broken Trust: Herbert Samuel, Zionism and the Palestinians 1920-1925 I.B.Tauris, 2001 p.57

Do you see how it works? Without Hitler and the slaughter of the Jews, Churchill and the Zionists could not get the support of the British people to go along with the apartheid that has been established in Palestine. Hitler did not drop out of the sky! He was financed by the elite. The British, American, and Zionist elitist financed Hitler. This is undisputable. No doubt about it! It is no secret that Grandpa Bush's clan was in bed with Hitler and his rise to power.

Refer to:
-Pool, James <u>Who Financed Hitler</u> Simon & Schuster Adult Publishing Group, 1997
-Sutton, Anthony <u>Wall Street and the Rise of Hitler</u> Buccaneer Books, Inc., 2007
-Black, Edwin <u>Nazi Nexus: America's Corporate Connections to Hitler's Holocaust</u> Dialog Press, 2008

Government documents show that Bush, the grandfather of President George W. Bush, was one of seven directors of Union Banking Corp., seized by the federal government because of its ties to a German industrialist who helped bankroll Adolf Hitler's rise to power, government

FEDERAL REGISTER, *Saturday, November 7, 1942* · 9097

and determining that to the extent that any or all of such nationals are persons not within a designated enemy country, the national interest of the United States requires that such persons be treated as nationals of the aforesaid designated enemy country or countries (Germany and/or Hungary), and having made all determinations and taken all action, after appropriate consultation and certification, required by said executive order or Act or otherwise, and deeming it necessary in the national interest, hereby vests such property in the Alien Property Custodian, to be held, used, administered, liquidated, sold or otherwise dealt with in the interest of and for the benefit of the United States.

Such property and any or all of the proceeds thereof shall be held in a special account pending further determination of the Alien Property Custodian. This shall not be deemed to limit the powers of the Alien Property Custodian to return such property or the proceeds thereof, or to indicate that compensation will not be paid in lieu thereof, if and when it should be determined that such return should be made or such compensation should be paid.

Any person, except a national of a designated enemy country, asserting any claim arising as a result of this order may file with the Alien Property Custodian a notice of his claim, together with a request for a hearing thereon, on Form APC–1, within one year from the date hereof, or within such further time as may be allowed by the Alien Property Custodian. Nothing herein contained shall be deemed to constitute an admission of the existence, validity or right to allowance of any such claim.

The terms "national", "designated enemy country" and "business enterprise within the United States" as used herein shall have the meanings prescribed in section 10 of said executive order.

Executed at Washington, D. C., on October 20, 1942.

[SEAL]

LEO T. CROWLEY,
Alien Property Custodian.

[F. R. Doc. 42–11568; Filed, November 6, 1942; 11:31 a. m.]

[Vesting Order Number 248]

ALL OF THE CAPITAL STOCK OF UNION BANKING CORPORATION AND CERTAIN INDEBTEDNESS OWING BY IT

Under the authority of the Trading with the enemy Act, as amended, and Executive Order No. 9095, as amended,[1] and pursuant to law, the undersigned, after investigation, finding:

(a) That the property described as follows:

All of the capital stock of Union Banking Corporation, a New York corporation, New York, New York, which is a business enterprise within the United States, consisting of 4,000 shares of $100 par value common capital stock, the names of the registered owners of which, and the number of shares owned by them respectively, are as follows:

Names	Number of shares
E. Roland Harriman	3,991
Cornelius Lievense	4
Harold D. Pennington	1
Ray Morris	1
Prescott S. Bush	1
H. J. Kouwenhoven	1
Johann G. Groeninger	1
Total	4,000

[1] 7 F.R. 5205.

all of which shares are held for the benefit of Bank voor Handel en Scheepvaart, N. V., Rotterdam, The Netherlands, which bank is owned or controlled by members of the Thyssen family, nationals of Germany and/or Hungary,

is property of nationals, and represents ownership of said business enterprise which is a national, of a designated enemy country or countries (Germany and/or Hungary);

(b) That the property described as follows:

All right, title, interest and claim of any name or nature whatsoever of the aforesaid Bank voor Handel en Scheepvaart, and August Thyssen-Bank, Berlin, Germany, and each of them, in and to all indebtedness, contingent or otherwise and whether or not matured, owing to them, or each of them, by said Union Banking Corporation, including but not limited to all security rights in and to any and all collateral for any or all of such indebtedness and the right to sue for and collect such indebtedness,

is an interest in the aforesaid business enterprise held by nationals of an enemy country or countries, and also is property within the United States owned or controlled by nationals of a designated enemy country or countries (Germany and/or Hungary);

- 117 -

Another thing to consider is this. George Herbert Walker and his son-in-law, Prescott Bush, were both very active in the emergence of the eugenics societies that were popular among the wealthy classes in the first half of the twentieth century. Prescott Bush was the Connecticut Director of the Mental Hygiene Society that originated at Yale University in 1908. The headquarters of the American Eugenics Society was also located at Yale University, which Prescott Bush and the two President George's attended. In 1952, the American Eugenics Society relocated and merged with the Population Council. One of the founders of the Population Council was none other than John D. Rockefeller. Another co-founder of the council was John Foster Dulles. Dulles was a lawyer for Brown Brothers Harriman, who as evidence shows had ties to the Nazi Party. John Foster Dulles was also a member of President Eisenhower's cabinet as the chief advisor. I mention all of this because it is a well established fact that the Nazis were big on eugenics. These people are demons in human skin. They really believe that they are gods and we are nothing but animals. Because they believe this is so, they are now attempting to manipulate our genetic make-up.

Prescott Bush and his bank was only one of the many American Corporations that helped finance Hitler. It is a well established fact that IBM helped finance Hitler and supplied Hitler with technology. The bar codes that you see on Holocaust survivors were produced by IBM. Hitler and the Nazi Party received funds from many so-called capitalist corporations. In 1925, the Hugo Stinnes family contributed funds to convert the Nazi weekly *Volkischer Beobachter* to a daily publication. Who was Hugo Stinnes? Hugo Stinnes (February 12, 1870 - April 10, 1924) was a German industrialist and rich politician born in Mülheim, in the Ruhr Valley, North German Confederation. During the 1920s, his fame flourished and his businesses soared. In 1923, the newly created *Time Magazine* called him "The New Emperor of Germany" to describe his far-reaching political influence and unimaginable wealth.

Hugo Stinnes

According to the Columbia Encyclopedia, Sixth Edition 2008, the Stinnes family owned enormous tracts of land in South America, including the largest oil concession in Argentina. It is no coincidence that Argentina took in many Nazi war criminals after World War II. The Stinnes also controlled part of the press and exercised financial power through their banks. World War I helped to expand their enterprises. After that war, the Stinnes took advantage of the German currency inflation and bought up businesses with worthless money. Hugo Stinnes was a founder of the German People's Party and was a member of the Reichstag.

ZBIGNIEW KAZIMIERZ BRZEZINSKI

Zbigniew Brzezinski is a prominent Polish-American political scientist who served under President Jimmy Carter as National Security Advisor from 1977 to 1981. The arming of the Mujahedeen (later known as al-Qaeda) in Afghanistan was done under Brzezinski. Brzezinski was also an advisor to the John F. Kennedy campaign during the 1960 presidential elections. In his book entitled *"The Grand ChessBoard"* Brzezinski states:

> *"Never before has a populist democracy attained international supremacy. But the pursuit of power is*

> *not a goal that commands popular passion, except*
> *in conditions of a sudden threat or challenge to the*
> *public's sense of domestic well-being. The economic*
> *self-denial (that is, defense spending) and the*
> *human sacrifice (casualties, even among*
> *professional soldiers) required in the effort are*
> *uncongenial to democratic instincts. Democracy is*
> *inimical to imperial mobilization." (p.35)*

This quote is somewhat of a microcosm of what has taken place over the last eight years. He is clearly in favor of military spending and sacrificing more soldiers to pursue power. This is very revealing stuff for the guy who is advising Barack Obama. Brzezinski is supposed to be a Democrat, and yet, in this 1997 book, he outlines what is to take place during the next Republican term in the Whitehouse under Bush and Cheney. It is important for you to understand the mentality of the character that is advising your next president. I feel comfortable in making that prediction because, not only is Barack Obama being supported and endorsed by Brzezinski, but he is also related to both Bush and Cheney by blood. The disclaimer to that prediction, however, will come to pass if Obama's true history is somehow leaked or revealed. The Unknowns are notorious for doing things like that in order to stir up racial tensions. Ignorant fools will believe it is the white man throwing dirt in Obama's eye. The truth of the matter is that Obama has already shown his true colors. He has also shown that Brzezinski's influence is apparent in his campaign rhetoric.

DISSING COUSINS: OBAMA, CHENEY, BUSH RELATED

By HASANI GITTENS
October 17, 2007

Who says Barack Obama doesn't have what it takes to be president? Turns out, he's a distant cousin of both Dick Cheney and George Bush. The vice president's wife, Lynne Cheney, announced her discovery yesterday while hawking her new book, "Blue Skies, No Fences," on MSNBC.

When asked if she would support Hillary Rodham Clinton because she is a woman, Lynne Cheney said, "I have to admit to a certain bias here . . . Dick and Barack Obama are eighth cousins."

Mrs. Cheney said that it was "an amazing American story that one ancestor . . . could be responsible down the family line for lives that have taken such different and varied paths." Then asked if she supported Obama she quickly said, "No."
Obama's camp made light of the family ties. "Every family has a black sheep," said spokeswoman Jen Psaki, with tongue firmly planted in cheek. The Chicago Sun-Times revealed the genealogical link in early September, claiming that the shared ancestors were Mareen and Susannah Duvall, 17th century immigrants from France.
The newspaper, however, claimed that the senator from Illinois and the vice president were 11th cousins.

The Duvalls are Obama's great-great-great-great-great-great-great-great-great-grandparents, and Cheney's great-great-great-great-great-great-great-great-grandparents, the paper said. George W. Bush and Obama, meanwhile, are 10th cousins once removed - linked through a 17th century Massachusetts couple, Samuel Hinckley and Sarah Soole, according to the Sun-Times.

This article can be found at
http://www.nypost.com/seven/10172007/news/regionalnews/dissing_co
usins__obama__cheney.htm as of 6/26/08

Many believe that the Bush administration is gearing up to strike Iran before the end of Bush's presidential term. This is highly unlikely due to the fact that the Bush administration has no more credibility left. I say this in light of what has been reported by prominent journalist Seymour Hersh concerning details of a plan allegedly devised by Vice President Dick Cheney. The plan gave details of how to provoke war with Iran. There is also a rumbling of an October surprise by Israel against Iran. This would make more sense because the plan that the elites have in place will continue under Obama. Obama has stated that Iran is a threat despite the fact that the Office of the Director of National Intelligence has stated that Iran halted its nuclear program in 2003 and has not started developing nuclear weapons as of 2007. In a November 2007 press release, the National Intelligence Office states:

> *"We assess with moderate confidence Tehran had not restarted its nuclear weapons program as of mid-2007, but we do not know whether it currently intends to develop nuclear weapons".*

Sources:
http://www.dni.gov/press_releases/2007120
3_release.pdf
http://www.youtube.com/watch?v=wxdL6w
YUWMM
http://www.youtube.com/watch?v=MDP8lXk1QSw

Obama claims that he is willing to sit down and talk with Iran. However, that is just a smoke screen to cover up the real intentions and plans that Brzezinski and the Council on Foreign Relations has set in motion for the Middle East.

The powers that be have exhausted the Bush administration's credibility. Therefore, once Obama is in office, you can expect another staged event that will be blamed on Iran (if Israel doesn't beat them to it). This will give Obama's administration the excuse needed to take out the threat that Obama calls Iran. This is why Obama will send the troops home from Iraq. He will send them home from Iraq—only to ship them off to Iran or Afghanistan. We cannot do simple mathematics anymore. Obama has publicly stated many times that he would like to concentrate more on Afghanistan. He has never shied away from that. Our ears hear the part about bringing the troops home from Iraq (with a timetable attached) but we cannot hear the part about sending them somewhere else.

You can read this article in it's entirety as of 7/1/08 at:
http://www.presstv.ir/detail.aspx?id=61626&sectionid=351020104

There is no credible evidence that Barack Obama, or anyone else, can show to prove that Iran is a threat to the United States or Israel—who both possess nuclear weapons. Iran is not known to possess any nukes. As a matter of fact, Iran has signed treaties renouncing possession of nuclear weapons. The treaties include the Biological Weapons Convention, the Chemical Weapons Convention, and the Nuclear Non-Proliferation Treaty (NPT). On ideological grounds, a public and categorical religious decree against the development, production, stockpiling, and use of nuclear weapons has been issued by the religious leader of Iran. A similar statement was made by the president of

Iran in an interview he had with NBC Nightly News anchor and managing editor, Brian Williams, in July of 2008.

Sources: http://www2.irna.ir/en/news/view/line-22/0711090297152426.htm
http://www.msnbc.msn.com/id/25884020/

Iran has repeatedly stated that its nuclear program is benevolent and to be used as a source of energy. The Russian Foreign Minister, Sergey Lavrov, has also stated that he has seen no evidence of any nuclear weapons program in Iran. What threat is Obama talking about? The only threat in the Middle East is Israel. Why? Because Israel is the only Middle Eastern country that most likely has nuclear weapons! Israel neither confirms nor denies it has nuclear weapons. However, Israeli Prime Minister Ehud Olmert had hinted, in a German television interview (in December 2006), that Israel did in fact have the bomb.

There is no proof that Iran wants to build a nuclear weapon. Such a weapon would be a violation of the Nuclear Non-Proliferation Treaty (NPT), which states that the nuclear program should be used only for civilian purposes. But did you know that Israel refuses to sign the Nuclear Non-Proliferation treaty?

The New York Times

Dispute Over Nuclear Treaty Is Souring Relations Between Israel and Egypt

By CHRIS HEDGES,
Published: February 24, 1995

Egypt, which in 1979 was the first Arab country to make peace with Israel, now sees an alarming deterioration of its relations with its neighbor, centered around a bitter <u>dispute over Israel's refusal to sign the treaty to prevent the spread of nuclear weapons.</u>

You can read this article in it's entirety as of 7/1/08 at:
http://query.nytimes.com/gst/fullpage.html?res=990CE4DD1F3AF937
A15751C0A963958260

Power players such as a Zbigniew Brzezinski are the reasons why a Barack Obama can appear out of nowhere and compete for the presidency of the United States. Obama is not one of us. By saying "not one of us," I do not mean black. I mean, he is not for the common folk or the average person. Obama is working for the power elite. Therefore, he will also push for a one world government. Why do I say that? I say that because his mentor and advisor, Zbigniew Brzezinski, believes it and promotes a one world state. Quoting his book "*The Grand Chessboard*" he states:

"In the long run, global politics are bound to become increasingly uncongenial to the concentration of hegemonic power in the hands of a single state. Hence, America is not only the first, as well as the only, truly global superpower, but it is also likely to be the very last." (p.209)

Zbigniew Brzezinski

To summarize Brzezinski, he is a member and former head of the Council on Foreign Relations, he co-created the Trilateral Commission, he believes in a one world government, he funded and helped create al-Qaeda, and of course, he feels that sacrificing soldiers in the great scheme of conquering sovereign lands is "A okay."

THE IBM CONNECTION

IBM was a major player in Hitler's empire. Information technology in the form of IBM's Hollerith punch-card machines provided the Nazis with a unique and critical tool in their task of cataloguing and dispatching their victims. IBM did not merely vend its products to Hitler, unlike many American companies, IBM also maintained a strategic alliance with Hitler's regime. IBM licensed and custom designed its products for use in the machinery of what is known as the Holocaust.

IBM typically responds to questions about its relationship with the Nazis by largely characterizing the information as old news. "The fact that Hollerith equipment manufactured by Dehomag (IBM's German unit) was used by the Nazi administration has long been known and is not new information," IBM representative Carol Makovich wrote in an email interview. This information was published in 1997 in The Institute of Electrical and Electronics Engineers (IEEE) Annals of the History of Computing. It was also published in Washington Jewish Week.

The Village Voice
Week of March 27 - April 2, 2002

How IBM Helped Automate the Nazi Death Machine in Poland

Final Solutions
by Edwin Black

> *When Adolf Hitler came to power in 1933, most of the world saw a menace to humanity. But IBM saw Nazi Germany as a lucrative trading partner. Its president, Thomas J. Watson, engineered a strategic business alliance between IBM and the Reich, beginning in the first days of the Hitler regime and continuing right through World War II. This alliance catapulted Nazi Germany to become IBM's most important customer outside the U.S. IBM and the Nazis jointly designed, and IBM exclusively produced, technological solutions that enabled Hitler to accelerate and in many ways automate key aspects of his persecution of Jews, homosexuals, Jehovah's Witnesses, and others the Nazis considered enemies. Custom-designed, IBM-produced punch*

cards, sorted by IBM machines leased to the Nazis, helped organize and manage the initial identification and social expulsion of Jews and others, the confiscation of their property, their ghettoization, their deportation, and, ultimately, even their extermination.

Recently discovered Nazi documents and Polish eyewitness testimony make clear that IBM's alliance with the Third Reich went far beyond its German subsidiary. A key factor in the Holocaust in Poland was IBM technology provided directly through a special wartime Polish subsidiary reporting to IBM New York, mainly to its headquarters at 590 Madison Avenue.
And that's how the trains to Auschwitz ran on time.

Thousands of IBM documents reviewed for the first edition of my book 'IBM and the Holocaust,' published early last year and focused mainly on IBM's German subsidiary, revealed vigorous efforts to preserve IBM's monopoly in the Nazi market and increase contracts to meet wartime sales quotas.

Since then, continued research and interviews have uncovered details, described here for the first time, of IBM's work for the Nazis in Poland through the separate subsidiary and of the Polish subsidiary's direct contact with IBM officials on Madison Avenue.

Documents were obtained from IBM files shipped to NYU for processing and from scores of other archival sources here and abroad. Not a single sentence written by IBM personnel has been discovered in any of the documents questioning the morality of automating the Third Reich, even when headlines proclaimed the mass murder of Jews.

IBM's German subsidiary was Deutsche Hollerith Maschinen Gesellschaft, known by the acronym Dehomag. (Herman Hollerith was the German American who first automated U.S. census information in the late 19th century and founded the company which became IBM. Hollerith's name became synonymous with the machines and the Nazi "departments" that operated them.) Watson tightly managed the lucrative German operation, traveling to Berlin at least twice annually from 1933 until 1939 to personally supervise Dehomag. Major German correspondence was translated for review by the New York office and often for Watson's personal comment. Before big new accounts were accepted, Watson had to assent. For deniability, he insisted on making direct verbal instructions to his German managers the rule rather than exception—even in place of major contracts. Once, when German managers wanted to paint a corridor, they awaited his specific permission. Watson's auditors continuously tracked the source and status of every reichsmark and pfennig—in one typical case, exchanging numerous transatlantic letters over the disposition of just a few dollars. Not infrequently, Dehomag managers objected to his "domination." Understandably, IBM's lawyers and managers in Berlin personally updated Watson constantly, and generally signed their reports, "Awaiting your further instructions."

No machines were sold to the Nazis—only leased. IBM was the sole source of all punch cards and spare parts, and it serviced the machines on-site—whether at Dachau or in the heart of Berlin—either directly or through its authorized dealer network or field trainees. There were no universal punch cards. Each series was custom-designed by IBM engineers not only to capture the information going in, but also to tabulate the information the Nazis wanted to come out.

IBM constantly updated its machinery and applications for the Nazis. For example, one series of punch cards was designed to record religion, national origin, and mother tongue, but by creating special columns and rows for Jew, Polish language, Polish nationality, the fur trade as an occupation, and then Berlin, Nazis could quickly cross-tabulate, at the rate of 25,000 cards per hour, exactly how many Berlin furriers were Jews of Polish extraction. Railroad cars, which could take two weeks to locate and route, could be swiftly dispatched in just 48 hours by means of a vast network of punch-card machines. Indeed, IBM services coursed through the entire German infrastructure in Europe.

This article can be read in it's entirety at:
http://www.villagevoice.com/2002-03-26/news/final-solutions/

If you think this is not possible today, you should think again. The Unknowns still continue with Hitler's plans. The European Union, or the Union of all European countries, was one of Hitler's goals. Even so, they pass it off (as they always do) as something benevolent. Meanwhile, countries continue to lose their sovereignty and are made to bow down to a foreign power.

Genetic manipulation and eugenics was another thing that the Nazis took seriously—as they worked on their master race bit. Today, IBM is still at it by way of their DNA data base.

Refer to
http://www.nytimes.com/2005/10/10/business/10gene.html?pagewanted =print 10oct2005

Many questions have been raised about using a DNA data base for employees. These demons do not change and their tactics do not change. They always get you to accept their agenda under the guise of protecting you. For the time being, the DNA database is only for the petty criminals. But who should be trusted with such data?

I can recall speaking with people over fifteen years ago concerning implantable microchips. Most people thought that I was crazy. I know many of you have heard about the so-called conspiracy theories regarding a government plan to implant people with microchips. I wonder if those people still believe that I am crazy, now that microchips are a reality. But of course, do not believe me, check it out!

Refer to: http://www.verichipcorp.com/
http://www.usatoday.com/news/washington/2003-04-15-dna-usat_x.htm

THE VERICHIP CORPORATION

VeriChip is the name of the company spear heading the implantable microchip technology. Do not be fooled into believing that this is a good thing because of the propaganda they have on their website. Do you really believe that they are going to tell you the chip is really made to further enslave you? They do what they have always done. They pass it off as something that is a luxury for you. Then they will pass it off as something that is for your safety. Lastly (check mate), they will pass it off as something that you will need in order to survive. In one scenario, you will not be able to buy or sell anything if your chip is not activated and working.

At first, they will keep the technology from the poor and make it accessible only to the wealthy or those in government. The same thing happened with credit cards. Early on, the credit cards were only for the rich and wealthy. I do not have to document how many people use credit cards nowadays. It all goes back to psychological warfare. They know how we think. Or better yet, they know how we have been trained to think. They know most people want what other people (who they consider successful, rich and powerful) have. However, their best strategy is to create a problem and get the people to react. After they get your reaction to that problem, then they offer the solution or the fix to the problem they created in the first place. This allows them to introduce laws and policies that people would ordinarily reject.

Today there is a push to collapse the dollar and plunge the United States into a new type of depression. The economy will continue to down spiral until they can introduce a new type of currency. The new currency will perhaps be the amero, which will almost assuredly be followed by a cashless society. The cashless society will be led by the microchips implanted in human beings. Your finances will be linked to this chip. If the powers that be need to freeze your account to get your attention, they will turn off your chip to let venders know that you are prohibited from buying or selling goods or services.

One need not be a rocket scientist to foresee the campaign they will use to convince the people that a microchipped population is a good thing. In the following article, you will see that the chip is already being implemented in just the manner I have described. You have government employees in Mexico being implanted and the young hot shot club hoppers in Spain are paying for drinks with their implantable chips. It is bad enough we have accepted their vaccinations. DO NOT ACCEPT THE MICROCHIP UNDER ANY CIRCUMSTANCES!!!!!!!

Posted 10/13/2004 10:17 AM   Updated 10/13/2004 1:46 PM

FDA approves use of implantable data chip

By Diedtra Henderson, Associated Press

WASHINGTON — The Food and Drug Administration on Wednesday approved
an implantable computer chip that can pass a patient's medical details
to doctors.

VeriChips, radio frequency microchips the size of a grain of rice, have already been used to identify wayward pets and livestock. And nearly 200 people working in Mexico's attorney general's office have been implanted with chips to control access to secure areas containing sensitive documents. Applied Digital Solutions (ADSX) of Delray Beach, Fla., in July asked the FDA for approval to use the implantable chip for medical uses in the United States. The agency had 60 days to reply.

In morning trading Wednesday, Applied Digital shares were up 92 cents at $3.04 on the Nasdaq Stock Market — near the middle of their 52-week range of $1.94 to $5. It's the first time the FDA has approved the use of the device, though in Mexico, more than 1,000 scannable chips have been implanted. The chip's serial number pulls up the patients' blood type and other medical information.

With the pinch of a syringe, the microchip is inserted under the skin in a procedure that takes less than 20 minutes and leaves no stitches. Silently and invisibly, the dormant chip stores a code — similar to the identifying UPC code on products sold in retail stores — that releases patient-specific information when a scanner passes over the chip. At the doctor's office those codes stamped onto chips, once scanned, would reveal such information as a patient's allergies and prior treatments.

The FDA in October 2002 said that the agency would regulate health care applications possible through VeriChip. Meanwhile, the chip has been used for a number of security-related tasks as well as for pure whimsy: <u>Club hoppers in Barcelona, Spain, now use the microchip much like a smartcard to speed drink orders and payment.</u>

The previous USA Today article can be found at: http://www.usatoday.com/money/industries/technology/2004-10-13-human-microchips_x.htm as of 4/17/08.

IBM is the company behind VeriChip, the major retailer of implantable chips. Keep in mind that IBM also ran the cataloging system used by the Nazis to store information. It was stored on the bar code you see on the arms of Jews during World War II. We are in serious danger! But as long as we only care about watching Survivor and American Idol, they will turn us into microchipped animals.

When the chip was not in existence, I was called a conspiracy theorist. This topic has travelled from conspiracy theory to a conspiracy fact. Nearly twenty years ago, I was talking about something that did not exist. Today the chip exists and people like me are still being called conspiracy theorists. Instead of doubting, the fool should be asking, "How did you know they were going to develop an implantable chip?"

As usual, the criminal elite will present the implantable chip as a good thing for society. They now claim the chip helps the doctors with their patients. They also promote that if your child has one, you will know where they are at all times. Therefore, no one will be able to kidnap your child. They will also insist that with the chip, you will be able to say goodbye to identity theft. Once they can microchip the population like animals, it would be a checkmate, game over!

Do not be surprised if a famous person's child gets kidnapped in order to take microchipping to the next level. It could also be the child of someone they plaster all over the news—just as they did with JonBenet Ramsey. They have already started testing the missing child strategy in Europe.

The following article is only in part. The whole document can be found at http://www.eurekamagazine.co.uk/article/10637/Rapid-response.aspx as of 4/17/08.

Eureka
Innovative Engineering Design

Rapid response   **13/08/2007**

Last month's 'appeal' to identify technologies that could prevent child abduction has moved forward rapidly

In a letter published last month, prompted by the disappearance of

Madeleine McCann, design engineer Peter Fitzsimmons challenged Eureka readers to come up with a device to track lost children. Several readers have written with suggestions – two RFID-based ideas, one of which is in production, are highlighted here. At the same time, two competing satellite-based systems – one British, one French – have also been launched recently.

Maidstone-based Blue Tree Services launched its OurKids child tracking system in the UK and Ireland earlier this year. The device comes in two parts: children wear the Blueranger unit, supplied with a belt similar to a money belt or with a pocket that can be attached to any item. Parents track their child's movements through BlueMap software either on the internet or via a hand-held PDA. The latter shows its location as well as that of the monitored units.

The portable units use GPS and the cell phone network to send positioning information – accurate within 4m – to secure servers. These then relay information, which shows the unit location within the UK or Europe.

Later in the article, it talks about the RFID chip being surgically implanted into children. Many of the teachers posted in the introduction page of this book have warned about these implantable chips for decades. In the 1980s they were also called conspiracy theorists. Today they are still being called conspiracy theorists because the chips are only here for our own good. Those who present the arguments in favor of the microchips are master manipulators. They know that most people abhor child abductions. This is why it will be a key issue in order to get you to comply. It will move from a luxury, to a law requiring you to get microchipped, or you will face being fined or imprisoned.

TRUTH ABOUT THE WAR ON DRUGS

Just Say No To Drugs! Who can forget that slogan? It is interesting that while good police officers risk their lives on the streets fighting petty drug dealers, big government agencies such as the DEA and CIA are keeping the police busy by shipping in the drugs. Drug users and local drug dealers do not own airplanes and boats to ship in the drugs. The media and Hollywood like to connect poor and oppressed people with drugs, but they rarely ever explain how the drugs get on the streets. The reality is that international drug trafficking requires cargo planes, landing strips (in several countries), networks of international links, an abundant source of investment money, networks for money laundering, and high-level associates for getting past U.S. customs and honest officers of the Drug Enforcement Agency (DEA).

In the August of 1996, a courageous investigative journalist by the name of Gary Webb wrote one of the first pieces of journalism that reached a massive audience—thanks in part to the Internet. He wrote an excellent 20,000 word, three-part series documenting the links between cocaine traffickers, the crack epidemic of the 1980s, and the CIA-organized right-wing Nicaraguan Contra Army of that epoch. The series ignited major interest in the social justice system concerning African-American communities. This interest led to street protests, constant discussion on black-oriented talk radio, and demands by congressional black caucus members for a federal investigation. But shortly after, Webb suffered a tremendous backlash at the hands of the national media, which was no doubt being spear headed by the powers that control it and the CIA.

There is no question that Gary Webb was murdered by these criminals. However, the official report states that Gary Webb allegedly committed suicide. His alleged suicide was as ridiculous and absurd as any suicide in recent history. We are expected to believe that he committed suicide by shooting himself in the head twice! How can you kill yourself by shooting yourself in the head twice? Do they expect us to believe that the first bullet had no affect? Or at least no affect to the point where he was conscious enough to squeeze the trigger again! How big and hard was his head? Apparently it was hard enough to withstand a blast at point blank range. This is so blatant and utterly insane! Even if you are using blanks, the pure pressure of the explosion is enough to kill you. Have you noticed that suspects (usually patsies) and people who expose the criminal elite tend to commit suicide?

Gary Webb exposed them and put the truth about the War on Drugs on the front burner. But what is this War on Drugs really about? It is about several things. One includes the prison business. People do not realize that prisons make big money. The inmates are lawfully enslaved under the Thirteenth Amendment, as they are forced to work for pennies on the dollar. This enables private corrections facilities to grow and receive investment dollars. A good example of this was demonstrated in *The Shawshank Redemption,* starring Morgan Freeman and Tim Robbins.

Gary Webb (1955-2004)

Amendment XIII

Section 1. Neither slavery nor involuntary servitude, **except as a punishment for crime whereof the party shall have been duly convicted, shall exist within the United States**, or any place subject to their jurisdiction.

In the November of 1993, Judge Robert C. Bonner, the former head of the DEA, told 60 Minutes that the CIA was allowing its assets to bring in tons of cocaine into the United States.

Source: http://www.csun.edu/coms/ben/news/cia/ven/60m.html

The CIA claimed it was conducting operations to track drugs coming into the United States and the only reason the drugs made it into the country was due to the agencies mismanagement of the drugs. In 1996 the former Venezuelan Anti-Narcotics Chief and CIA asset, General Ramon Guillen Davila, was indicted by a Miami court for leading a CIA led counter-narcotics program that smuggled several tons of cocaine into the United States. The Venezuelan Government refused to extradite

Mr. Davila and even granted him a pardon of any crimes he may have committed while serving his office. According to Mr. Davila and the Venezuelan Government, the drugs were acquired from the Colombian drug cartels of Cali and smuggled into the United States and Europe with the approval of the CIA. Ramon Guillen Davila is the same CIA asset that Hugo Chavez's administration alleged was being used by the Bush administration to assassinate the Venezuelan President, Hugo Chavez. As a side note, Ramon Davila was also a graduate of the infamous "School of the Americas." (More on this school later)

> ***Sources***: http://www.venezuelanalysis.com/news/2264
> Cockburn, Alexander & St.Clair Jeffery, Whiteout (The C.I.A.,
> Drugs and the Press) Verso 1998.

The fact that the CIA has been smuggling drugs into the United States is not even a secret. It is so well documented that even the mainstream media has reported on it. The only reason why our streets are over flowing with drugs is because it is allowed by the powers that be. If they did not want any drugs in the United States, then there would be no drugs in the United States! It is wake up time!!

SFGate

home of the
San Francisco Chronicle

What Will Congress Do About New CIA-Drug Revelations?

Peter Dale Scott

Monday, June 19, 2000

CONGRESS WILL shortly have to decide whether to bury or deal with explosive new revelations that the Central Intelligence Agency protected major drug traffickers who aided the Contra army in Central America. These new findings go far beyond the original stories which gave rise to them by Gary Webb in 1996. Webb had alleged that cocaine from two Contra-supporting traffickers, Norwin Meneses and

Danilo Blandon, had helped fuel the national crack epidemic. The resulting political firestorm brought promises of a full investigation. After an unprecedented review of internal CIA and Justice Department files, three massive reports, totaling almost 1,000 pages, were released by the inspectors general of the CIA (Fred Hitz) and Justice Department (Michael Bromwich). The new revelations confirmed many of Webb's claims. Meneses and Blandon were admitted to have been (despite previous press denials) ``significant traffickers who also supported, to some extent, the Contras.'' For years they escaped prosecution, until after support for the Contras ended.

Meanwhile the reports opened the doors on worse scandals. According to the reports, the CIA made conscious use of major traffickers as agents, contractors and assets. It maintained good relations with Contras it knew to be working with drug traffickers. It protected traffickers which the Justice Department was trying to prosecute, sometimes by suppressing or denying the existence of information. This protection extended to major Drug Enforcement Agency targets considered to be among the top smugglers of cocaine into this country. Perhaps the most egregious example is that of the Honduran trafficker Juan Ramon Matta Ballesteros. Matta had been identified by the DEA in 1985 as the most important member of a consortium moving a major share (perhaps a third, perhaps more than half) of all the cocaine from Colombia to the United States. The DEA also knew that Matta was behind the kidnapping of a DEA agent in Mexico, Enrique Camarena, who was subsequently tortured and murdered.

A public enemy? Yes. But Matta was also an ally of the CIA. Matta's airline, SETCO, was recorded in U.S. files as a drug-smuggling airline. It was also the chief airline with which the CIA contracted to fly supplies to the Contra camps in Honduras. When the local DEA office began to move against Matta in 1983, it was shut down. Though Matta's whereabouts were well-known, the United States did not arrest and extradite him until 1988, a few days after Congress ended support for the Contras.

At Matta's first drug trial, a U.S. attorney described him as ``on the level of the top 10 Colombian drug traffickers.'' We now learn from the CIA Hitz reports that, in the same year, 1989, CIA officials reported falsely, in response to an inquiry from Justice, that in CIA files ``There are no records of a SETCO Air.'' CIA officers appear also to have lied to Hitz's investigators about who said this.

There appears to have been a broad pattern of withholding information from the Justice Department. For example, when Justice began to investigate the drug activities of two Contra supporters, CIA *headquarters turned down proposals that CIA should interview the two men. The reason in one case was that such documentation would be ``exactly the sort of thing the U.S. Attorney's Office will be investigating.'' The House Committee on Intelligence received this information, and chose to deny it. According to a recent committee report, ``There is no evidence . . . that CIA officers . . . ever concealed narcotics trafficking information or allegations involving the Contras.''*

Just as dishonestly, the committee found that ``there is unambiguous reporting in the CIA materials reviewed showing that the Nicaraguan Democratic Force (FDN) leadership in Nicaragua would not accept drug monies and would remove from its ranks those who had involvement in drug trafficking.'' In fact, the Hitz reports contained a detailed account of drug-trafficking by members of the main FDN faction, the September 15th League (ADREN). Those named included the FDN chief of logistics. According to the Hitz Reports, ``CIA also received allegations or information concerning drug trafficking by nine Contra-related individuals in the (FDN) Northern Front.'' This included credible information, corroborated elsewhere, against leaders such as Juan Ramon Rivas, the Northern Army chief of staff. Yet CIA support for the FDN continued, through a period when aid to any drug-tainted Contra organization was forbidden by statute.

In short, the House Committee Report is a dishonest coverup of CIA wrong-doings, what one might expect from a committee chaired and staffed by former CIA officers.

As committee member Congresswoman Nancy Pelosi, D-S.F., said in a hearing two years ago, ``This is an issue of great concern in our community.'' Will she, and other like-minded representatives, repudiate this flimsy attempt to silence that concern with falsehoods?''

The answer may depend on the voters: Will they object as strongly as before?

Peter Dale Scott was an expert witness before the Citizens' Commission on U.S. Drug Policy.

Refer to:
http://www.sfgate.com/cgi-bin/article.cgi?file=/chronicle/archive/2000/06/19/ED58466.DTL

Confidence Games

Monday, Nov. 29, 1993
By HOWARD G. CHUA-EOAN

Weighing in at 998 lbs., the shipment of cocaine that slipped into the country through Miami International Airport in late 1990 was large but not extraordinary. The clues to its origins, however, were tantalizing. The U.S. Customs Service, which discovered and confiscated the drugs, learned from Venezuela's secret police that their country's National Guard was behind the contraband. Joining the probe, the U.S. Drug Enforcement Administration made an even more surprising discovery: the shipment was under the direct supervision of General Ramon Guillen Davila, Venezuela's top drug fighter and a close collaborator with U.S. counternarcotics operations. And it was not the first such shipment. Earlier ones totaling nearly 2,000 lbs. had already made their way onto the streets of American cities. A DEA investigation then uncovered a scandal in which a fellow U.S. agency, the CIA, may have unwittingly helped Venezuelan paramilitary officers run a profitable coke-trafficking operation. Details of the scheme emerged last week as the CIA, prompted by reports that TV's 60 Minutes was preparing an expose, acknowledged that its actions in Venezuela were "regrettable" and the result of "poor judgment." Says one DEA official, "They got caught with their pants down." The DEA investigated a key meeting in December 1989, when CIA officer Mark McFarlin and his boss Jim Campbell, the CIA station chief in Venezuela, met with Annabelle Grimm, attache of the DEA in Caracas. McFarlin, who was assigned to coordinate counternarcotics operations with Guillen's National Guard antidrug unit, wanted Grimm's assistance. He asked her to allow hundreds of pounds of cocaine to be shipped to the U.S. through Venezuela. And he asked that the DEA make sure the contraband would not be interdicted -- in other words, "let the dope walk."

The stated purpose of the scheme was to help one of the Venezuelan general's agents win the confidence of Colombia's drug lords. It would also help the CIA and the DEA gather crucial information about the cartel's methods. But Grimm refused to cooperate. As she later told 60 Minutes: "I really take great exception to the fact that 1,000 kilos came in funded by U.S. taxpayer money." Besides, said DEA agents, they already had enough information about the Medellin cartel's activities. They did not need a "cockamamie" scheme to distribute tons of drugs to gain a little more color. Guillen was undeterred. His agents took delivery of drugs from Colombia and stored them in a truck at the CIA-funded counternarcotics center near Caracas. Several caches were then flown off to the U.S., and all went well -- until the Miami bust in late 1990. According to DEA sources, McFarlin allegedly shared information with Guillen that the Venezuelan secret police were on to the scheme. The shipments continued, however, until Guillen tried to send in 3,373 lbs. of cocaine at once. The DEA, watching closely, stopped it and pounced.

Found as of 8/1/08:
http://www.time.com/time/magazine/article/0,9171,979669,00.html?iid=chix-sphere

Published: Nov. 30, 1996

BY DAVID LaGESSE AND GEORGE RODRIGUE
Dallas Morning News

WASHINGTON -- Ten years ago, El Salvador's Ilopango Air Base served as the major depot for American aid pouring south into a secret war against Nicaragua's Marxist Sandinista regime. A former federal agent charges that Ilopango also served as a key transit point for smugglers flying narcotics back north, some of whom flew for the U.S.-backed Contras.

Former Drug Enforcement Administration Agent Celerino Castillo III said that while the White House ran its covert war, he ran his own secret operation -- and that his informants found a startling mix of arms, narcotics and money at Ilopango. Castillo, now retired and living in McAllen, Texas, said he found that many pilots flying for the Contras were listed in DEA records as suspected smugglers.

"I found that other agencies were sleeping with my enemy," Castillo said in a recent interview. "They knew these guys (pilots) were suspected drug traffickers, and hired them anyway." Former officials at the base deny permitting or condoning smuggling. "It is absolutely false and all ... (expletive)," said former CIA agent Felix Rodriguez, who ran the Contra resupply effort at Ilopango for the Reagan White House's National Security Council.

... When Castillo first published his allegations, in a 1994 book titled "Powderburns," they got little attention. More recent allegations of possible CIA complicity in the cocaine trade, made most prominently by the Mercury News, have raised new interest in Castillo's account. During a Senate Intelligence Committee hearing last week, members of the audience shouted demands for an investigation of the Texan's charges.

... Information gathered by the Dallas Morning News in Washington, Texas, Panama and El Salvador indicates that during his Central American service Castillo was rated as a dedicated and capable agent and that he had grounds for thinking that the United States was knowingly working with smugglers. The Dallas Morning News spoke

with Castillo's informants, with some of his supervisors and with an accused smuggler who flew out of Ilopango. The paper also reviewed previous congressional hearing records and some still-secret government documents by and about Castillo.

Castillo's two chief informants had intimate knowledge of Ilopango and its military overseers. They had access to its records. And they confirmed that they told Castillo that the airport was often used by drug smugglers and by drug-money couriers.

..."Castillo's stuff about Ilopango fits," said John Mattes, a former investigator for the Senate Subcommittee on Terrorism, Narcotics and International Communications. Its chairman, Sen. John Kerry, D-Mass., probed Contra smuggling allegations in the late 1980s.

The former agent of the United States Drug Enforcement Administration named in the previous articles made a written statement to the House Permanent Select Committee on Intelligence.

WRITTEN STATEMENT OF CELERINO CASTILLO III, (D.E.A., RETIRED) FOR THE HOUSE PERMANENT SELECT COMMITTEE ON INTELLIGENCE
April 27, 1998

For several years, I fought in the trenches of the front lines of Reagan's "Drug War", trying to stamp out what I considered American's greatest foreign threat. But, when I was posted, in Central and South America from 1984 through 1990, I knew we were playing the "Drug War Follies." While our government shouted "Just Say No !", entire Central and South American nations fell into what are now known as, "Cocaine democracies."

While with the DEA, I was able to keep journals of my assignments in Central and South America. These journals include names, case file numbers and DEA NADDIS (DEA Master Computer) information to back up my allegations. I have pictures and original passports of the victims that were murdered by CIA assets. These atrocities were done with the approval of the agencies.

We, ordinary Americans, cannot trust the C.I.A. Inspector General to conduct a full investigation into the CIA or the DEA. Let me tell you why. When President Clinton (June, 1996) ordered The Intelligence Oversight Board to conduct an investigation into allegations that US Agents were involved in atrocities in Guatemala, it failed to investigate several DEA and CIA operations in which U.S. agents knew before hand that individuals (some Americans) were going to be murdered.

I became so frustrated that I forced myself to respond to the I.O.B report citing case file numbers, dates, and names of people who were murdered. In one case (DEA file # TG-86-0005) several Colombians and Mexicans were raped, tortured and murdered by CIA and DEA assets, with the approval of the CIA. Among those victims identified was Jose Ramon Parra-Iniguez, Mexican passport A-GUC-043 and his two daughters Maria Leticia Olivier-Dominguez, Mexican passport A-GM-8381. Also included among the dead were several Colombian nationals: Adolfo Leon Morales-Arcilia "a.k.a." Adolfo Morales-Orestes, Carlos Alberto Ramirez, and Jiro Gilardo-Ocampo. Both a DEA and a CIA agent were present, when these individuals were being interrogated (tortured). The main target of that case was a Guatemalan Congressman, (Carlos Ramiro Garcia de Paz) who took delivery of 2,404 kilos of cocaine in Guatemala just before the interrogation. This case directly implicated the Guatemalan Government in drug trafficking (The Guatemalan Congressman still has his US visa and continues to travel at his pleasure into the US).

To add salt to the wound, in 1989 these murders were investigated by the U.S Department of Justice, Office of Professional Responsibility. DEA S/I Tony Recevuto determined that the Guatemalan Military Intelligence, G-2 (the worst human rights violators in the Western Hemisphere) was responsible for these murders. Yet, the U.S. government continued to order U.S. agents to work hand-in-hand with the Guatemalan Military. This information was never turned over to the I.O.B. investigation.

On October 5, 1989, the New York Times reported on the testimony of Assistant Treasury Secretary Salvatore R. Martoche to the Senate Subcommittee on Terrorism, Narcotics, and International Operations. The Martoche's testimony revealed that a papa Bush administration official admitted that U.S. banks were laundering the enormous sum of $110 billion a year in drug money. There is a war on drugs. What the people do not realize is that the war consists of making sure the drugs make their way into your homes and the lives of your children. If you are drugged up, how can you have the mental capacity to face your enemy? They know what they are doing. Ronald Reagan was the president that was supposed to wage this infamous War on Drugs. It is no coincidence that the crack epidemic took place during his presidency. As stated before, when ever they tell you that they are going to do something, you can almost always expect the exact opposite. For example, the War on Drugs pro-duced more drugs, the war on literacy produced more illiteracy and a dumbed down population. And now, the War on Terror has produced more terror.

This is a constant theme. Doesn't it seem like every politician talks about health care? Why is it, that health care for people in the United States keeps regressing? Getting medical attention is getting difficult for most working class families. When will we say "enough is enough?" When will we learn that these devils are all interconnected? There is no difference be-tween, Clinton, Bush, Obama, Nixon, Kissinger, Rockefeller, McCain, L.B.Johnson, Blair, and yada-yada-yada!

When will we stop isolating these administrations? They always reveal some truth years after the event has occurred and the alleged culprits are no longer in office. They know that you have moved on from that event and will not equate the perpe-trators to the current persons in office. Therefore the average person sees the fact that they allowed the Japanese to attack Pearl Harbor and kill our servicemen as a thing of the past. Many people reacted the same way when they learned of the planned terror attacks (Operation Northwoods) against American citizens to create a pretext for war against Cuba. The same applies to the attack of our servicemen on the USS Liberty (Refer to *The War on Terror Fraud*). People believe that these events are not connected to today. We just write these things off as being in the past. All they have done is changed actors, but the movie is still the same. Wake up! These demons do not care about you! It does not matter what the color of your skin is, your social status, your height, weight, or how many pretty clothes you have in your closet.

For the most part, the intellectual community has a sense of all this information. Good intelligent people normally reject these logical truths or ideas because the mainstream image of a conspiracy usually challenges the concept that most educated, intelligent people have about how the world elite really operate. Sometimes when confronted with something even remotely plausible, it may remind them of perhaps a past conspiracy that turned out to be unfounded and utterly incorrect. This is the very thing that typically breeds prejudice among most scholars and researchers. Even when they mistakenly uncover an operation or conspiracy within their own research, they often feel duty-bound, probably out of a sense of not being lumped in with the conspiracy nut, to sugar coat their research in an attempt to fit something that will not fall along the lines of a conspiracy accusation.

OPERATION MOCKINGBIRD

Operation Mockingbird was a CIA operation to basically buy domestic and foreign news media. This covert operation was made public during the Church Committee investigation of 1975 (published 1976). I would say that they have truly accomplished this task. According to the Congress report published in 1976, the following was revealed:

> "The CIA currently maintains a network of sever-
> al hundred foreign individuals around the world
> who provide intelligence for the CIA and at times
> attempt to influence opinion through the use of
> covert propaganda. These individuals provide the
> CIA with direct access to a large number of news-
> papers and periodicals, scores of press services

and news agencies, radio and television stations, commercial book publishers, and other foreign media outlets."

According to the Family Jewels report released by the National Security Archive on June 26, 2007, the CIA put taps on the phones of at least two Washington-based news reporters for a three month period covering March 12, 1963, through June 15, 1963. This type of surveillance on journalist was called Operation CELOTEX I-II. The Family Jewels report also reveals a document describing one of the founders and members of The Beatles, John Lennon, funding anti-war activists. John Lennon was well known as a peace activist who was against the Vietnam War.

The paper trail to support that the CIA or FBI played an integral part in the assassination of John Lennon is a bit on the thin side. However, Mark David Chapman, the man who was charged with the murder, had a Hawaii to New York airline ticket departing December 5th that was found in his hotel room by the authorities. Chapman had actually bought a Hawaii to Chicago ticket that was scheduled to depart on December 2nd with no connecting flight. The ticket found after he was taken into custody was apparently altered. Not one of his friends had knowledge of Chapman's trip to New York. They were under the impression that he went to Chicago for three days. One of the biggest coincidences of this case was the fact that he was assigned the same defense psychiatrist who diagnosed the assassin of Robert F. Kennedy. Dr. Bernard Diamond quickly labeled Chapman as a "Paranoid schizophrenic."

Here is a doozie. Most people in the United States have three names—first, middle, and last. Why is it that famous assassins are commonly known by all three of those names? This is a psychological tactic that is used in order to give you a personal relationship to these pawns. It is the same psychological doctrine used by attorneys. When defense attorneys deal with dead victims at trial, they avoid using the victim's actual name in court to avoid giving the victim sympathy from the jury.

John Wilkes Booth
(Lincoln)
Lee Harvey Oswald
(JFK)

Mark David Chapman
(Lennon)
James Earl Ray
(MLK)

John Wilkes Booth   Lee Harvey Oswald

These criminals are personalized in order to shift any suspicion away from a cover-up or conspiracy. Psych warfare has been a huge success for the Unknowns.

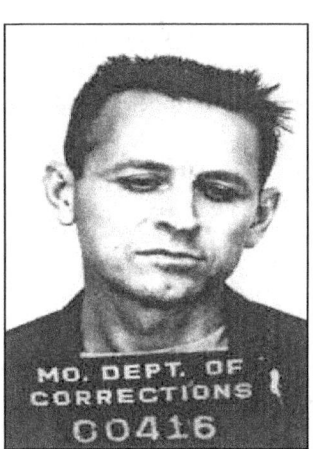

Mark David Chapman   James Earl Ray

HUGE C.I.A. OPERATION REPORTED IN U.S. AGAINST ANTIWAR FORCES, OTHER DISSIDENTS IN NIXON YEARS

Richard Helms   James R. Schlesinger   William E. Colby

FILES ON CITIZENS

Helms Reportedly Got Surveillance Data in Charter Violation

By SEYMOUR M. HERSH
Special to The New York Times

WASHINGTON, Dec. 21—The Central Intelligence Agency, directly violating its charter, conducted a massive, illegal domestic intelligence operation during the Nixon Administration against the antiwar movement and other dissident groups in the United States,

Seymour Hersh broke the story of the CIA's illegal domestic operations with a front page story in the *New York Times* on December 22, 1974.

John Lennon was not the only person being wire-tapped. The fact that the CIA has been wire-tapping American citizens is old news. Only those of you who do not know that you are slaves are surprised by such a revelation. They have committed far worse atrocities.

In November of 1962, according to the before mentioned Family Jewels report, the CIA also had plans to assassinate the then Congo leader, Patrice Lumumba. The plan was to kill Lumumba by way of poisoning him. According to ex-CIA chief, John Stockwell, this is common practice for CIA criminals.

John Stockwell is probably the highest-ranking CIA official to ever leave the agency and go public concerning its treacherous acts. Mr. Stockwell oversaw a CIA intelligence-gathering post in Vietnam. He was also the task-force commander of the CIA's secret war in Angola from 1975 to 1976. He was awarded the Medal of Merit just prior to his resignation. Stockwell's book, "*In Search of Enemies*" published by W.W. Norton in 1978, was an international best seller. In a lecture given by Mr. John Stockwell in October of 1987, he stated the following:

Note: The lecture appears here in part(s): *Take note that words in parenthesis have been inserted by the author and are not part of the original lecture.*

-What I found with all of this study is that the subject, the problem, if you will, for the world, for the U.S. is much, much, much graver, astronomically graver, than just Angola and Vietnam. I found that the Senate Church committee has reported, in their study of covert actions, that the CIA ran several thousand covert actions since 1961, and that the heyday of covert action was before 1961; that we have run several hundred covert actions a year, and the CIA has been in business for a total of 37 years.

- What we're going to talk about tonight is the United States national security syndrome. We're going to talk about how and why the U.S. manipulates the press. We're going to talk about how and why the U.S. is pouring money into El Salvador, and preparing to invade Nicaragua; how all of this concerns us so directly. I'm going to try to explain to you the other side of terrorism; that is, the other side of what Secretary of State Shultz talks about. In doing this, we'll talk about the Korean War, the Vietnam War, and the Central American war.

- Everything I'm going to talk to you about is represented, one way or another, already in the public records. You can dig it all out for yourselves, without coming to hear me if you so chose. Books, based on information gotten out of the CIA under the freedom of information act, testimony before the Congress, hearings before the Senate Church committee, research by scholars, witness of people throughout the world who have been to these

target areas that we'll be talking about. I want to emphasize that my own background is profoundly conservative. We come from South Texas, East Texas....

- I had been designated as the task-force commander that would run this secret war [in Angola in 1975 and 1976].... and what I figured out was that in this job, I would sit on a sub-committee of the National Security Council, this office that Larry Devlin has told me about where they had access to all the information about Angola, about the whole world, and I would finally understand national security. And I couldn't resist the opportunity to know. I knew the CIA was not a worthwhile organization, I had learned that the hard way. But the question was where did the U.S. Government fit into this thing, and I had a chance to see for myself in the next big secret war....

-I wanted to know if wise men were making difficult decisions based on truly important, threatening information, threatening to our national security interests. If that had been the case, I still planned to get out of the CIA, but I would know that the system, the invisible government, our national security complex, was in fact justified and worth while. (Most of the men and women in our intelligence agencies are good people who think the same way Mr. Stockwell just explained.) *And so I took the job.... Suffice it to say I wouldn't be standing in front of you tonight if I had found these wise men making these tough decisions. What I found, quite frankly, was fat old men sleeping through sub-committee meetings of the NSC in which we were making decisions that were killing people in Africa. I mean literally. Senior ambassador Ed Mulcahy... would go to sleep in nearly every one of these meetings....*

-You can change the names in my book [about Angola] [13] and you've got Nicaragua.... the basic structure, all

the way through including the mining of harbors, we addressed all of these issues. The point is that the U.S. led the way at every step of the escalation of the fighting. We said it was the Soviets and the Cubans that were doing it. It was the U.S. that was escalating the fighting. There would have been no war if we hadn't gone in first. We put arms in, they put arms in. We put advisors in, they answered with advisors. We put in Zairian para-commando battalions, they put in Cuban army troops. We brought in the S. African army; they brought in the Cuban army. And they pushed us away. They blew us away because we were lying, we were covering ourselves with lies, and they were telling the truth. And it was not a war that we could fight. We didn't have interests there that should have been defended that way.

- Now, the most significant thing that I got out of all of this, in addition to the fact that our rationales were basically false, was that we lied. To just about everybody involved. One third of my staff in this task force that I put together in Washington, commanding this global operation, pulling strings all over the world to focus pressure onto Angola, and military activities into Angola, one third of my staff was propagandists, who were working, in every way they could to create this picture of Cubans raping Angolans, Cubans and Soviets intro-ducing arms into the conflict, Cubans and Russians trying to take over the world.

- He (C.I.A. director Bill Colby) *lied about our relation-ship with South Africa. We were working closely with the South African army, giving them our arms, coordinating battles with them, giving them fuel for their tanks and armored cars. He said we were staying well away from them. They were concerned about these white merce-naries that were appearing in Angola, a very sensitive*

issue, hiring whites to go into a black African country, to help you impose your will on that black African country by killing the blacks, a very sensitive issue. The Congress was concerned we might be involved in that, and he assured them we had nothing to do with it.

-The Frank Snep ruling of the Supreme Court gave the government the right to sue a government employee for damages. If s/he writes an unauthorized account of the government which means the people who are involved in corruption in the government, who see it, who witness it, like Frank Snep did, like I did - if they try to go public they can now be punished in civil court. The government took $90,000 away from Frank Snep, his profits from his book, and they've seized the profits from my own book....

-[Reagan passed] the Intelligence Identities Protection act, which makes it a felony to write articles revealing the identities of secret agents or to write about their activities in a way that would reveal their identities. Now, what does this mean? In a debate in Congress - this is very contro- versial - the supporters of this bill made it clear.... If agents Smith and Jones came on this campus, in an MK- ultra-type experiment, and blew your fiancé's head away with LSD, it would now be a felony to publish an article in your local paper saying, `watch out for these 2 turkeys, they're federal agents and they blew my loved one's head away with LSD'. It would not be a felony what they had done because that's national security and none of them were ever punished for those activities......................

-Efforts to muzzle government employees. President Reagan has been banging away at this one ever since. Proposing that every government employee, for the rest of his or her life, would have to submit anything they wrote to 6 committees of the government for censorship, for the

*rest of their lives. To keep the scandals from leaking out...
to keep the American people from knowing what the
government is really doing...*

*-Then it starts getting heavy. The `Pre-emptive Strikes'
bill. President Reagan, working through the Secretary of
State Shultz... almost 2 years ago, submitted the bill that
would provide them with the authority to strike at
terrorists before terrorists can do their terrorism. But this
bill... provides that they would be able to do this in this
country as well as overseas. It provides that the secretary
of state would put together a list of people that he
considers to be terrorist, or terrorist supporters, or
terrorist sympathizers. And if your name, or your
organization, is put on this list, they could kick down your
door and haul you away, or kill you, without any due
process of the law and search warrants and trial by jury,
and all of that, with impunity.* (Does this sound familiar?
Of course it does! He is talking about the Patriot Act in a
different time, under another name. Keep in mind that the
Patriot Act was passed as something that was good for the
people. Who in their right mind thinks that it is good to be
hauled away or killed without even being charged with a
crime?)...................

*-Now, there was a tremendous outcry on the part of
jurists. The New York Times columns and other newspapers saying, `this is no different from Hitler's "night in
fog" program', where the government had the authority
to haul people off at night. And they did so by the thousands. And President Reagan and Secretary Shultz have
persisted.... Shultz has said, `Yes, we will have to take
action on the basis of information that would never stand
up in a court. And yes, innocent people will have to be
killed in the process. But, we must have this law because
of the threat of international terrorism'.* (Do you see why

they needed 9/11? Is the picture of Problem, Reaction, Solution getting clearer? Without a tragedy, Red Ronnie's (Ronald Regan) version of the Patriot Act took a lot of heat.)

-Think a minute. What is `the threat of international terrorism'? These things catch a lot of attention. But how many Americans died in terrorist actions last year? According to Secretary Shultz, 79. Now, obviously that's terrible but we killed 55,000 people on our highways with drunken driving; we kill 2,500 people in far nastier, bloodier, mutilating, gang-raping ways in Nicaragua last year alone ourselves. Obviously 79 peoples' death is not enough reason to take away the protection of American citizens, of due process of the law...........................

-But they're pressing for this. The special actions teams that will do the pre-emptive striking have already been created, and trained in the defense department. (Keep in mind that this is George W. Bush's policy. His policy is "Strike the terrorist first").......................................

They're building detention centers. There were 8 kept as mothballs under the McLaren Act after World War II, to detain aliens and dissidents in the next war, as was done in the next war, as was done with the Japanese people during World War II. They're building 10 more, and army camps, and the....... executive memos about these things say it's for aliens and dissidents in the next national emergency....

-FEMA, the Federal Emergency Management Agency, headed by Loius Guiffrida, a friend of Ed Meese's.... He's going about the country lobbying and demanding that he be given authority, in the times of national emergency, to declare martial law, and establish a curfew, and gun

down people who violate the curfew...... in the United States.

-And then there's Ed Meese, as I said. The highest law enforcement officer in the land, President Reagan's closest friend, going around telling us that the Constitution never did guarantee freedom of speech and press, and due process of the law, and (freedom of) *assembly...........................*

-What they are planning for this society and this is why they're determined to take us into a war if we'll permit it... is the Reagan revolution.... So he's getting himself some laws so when he puts in the troops in Nicaragua, he can take charge of the American people, and put people in jail, and kick in their doors, and kill them if they don't like what he's doing....

SCHOOL OF THE AMERICAS

Like much of the groups and historical events in this book, the average American is oblivious to the School of the Americas. Today the school is known as The Western Hemisphere Institute for Security Cooperation (WHISC).

This school has basically taught most of the dictators that have passed through South America. The current WHISC, now part of the United States Department of Defense, was originally created as part of the National Defense Authorization Act passed by Congress in 2001. It is estimated that over 60,000 Latin American soldiers and policemen have been trained since the school was created in 1946. Some of the notable names that have passed through this school are Generals Leopoldo Galtieri or Manuel Noriega, dictators such as Bolivia's Hugo Banzer, as well as some of Augusto Pinochet's officers. Luis Posada Carriles (well known as a terrorist) was educated by the school in 1961, although he never graduated.

The schools training manuals contain instructions in motivation by fear, bounties for enemy dead, false imprisonment, torture, execution, and kidnapping a targets family member(s). In other words, this training is no different than what the Colombian FARC or the Colombian paramilitary (an arm of the regular military) is doing in Colombia. It is also the same thing that is happening in Guantanamo Bay. The demons that pass through this school are entrusted to make countries in South America remain in a state of disarray. Meanwhile the natural resources in South American countries are controlled by foreign banks and corporations.

SCHOOL FOR SCANDAL
The School of the Americas,
at Georgia's Fort Benning,
became the target of protests
as war ravaged Central America
in the 1980s.

School of the Americas
Cold War training camp remains focus of controversy

By Bruce Kennedy
CNN Interactive

(CNN) -- The intruder waited in his hiding place for just the right moment -- soon after his targets had gone to bed. He then put his plan into operation.

Earlier that day in 1983, Vietnam veteran and priest Roy Bourgeois had walked unchallenged into Fort Benning, Georgia, wearing surplus military fatigues. He had climbed up a tree near a barracks used by Salvadoran soldiers training with the U.S. Army, waited until "lights out," then unleashed his guerrilla protest.

Bourgeois turned on his electronic "boom box" that blared into the night air a recording of Salvadoran Archbishop Oscar Romero calling on his nation's soldiers to stop killing their countrymen. Romero was later killed while conducting Mass in San Salvador. Of the three men accused in Romero's assassination, two were graduates of the U.S. Army's School of the Americas (SOA).

Bourgeois served 18 months in a federal prison for his actions. But his protest paved the way for larger demonstrations against what some people call the "School of Assassins" -- but what SOA supporters say is an important tool in helping spread democratic values to Washington's allies in Central America and South America.

The end of World War II and the start of the Cold War ignited new concerns in the United States that Communists would attempt to infiltrate and subvert the country's southern neighbors. The U.S. Army started its School of the Americas in Panama in 1946. In 1984, under the terms of the 1977 Panama Canal Treaty, the school was moved to Fort Benning.

More than 63,000 Central and South American soldiers from 22 nations have trained at SOA since its inception. According to the school's Web site, instruction at SOA for its first several decades "focused on nation-building skills, then [was] altered in 1961 by President John F. Kennedy to provide instruction necessary to the nations in Latin America to thwart armed communist insurgencies."

Opponents of the school, who maintain their own "School of the Americas Watch" Web site, claim SOA graduates "have been responsible for some of the worst human rights abuses in Latin America."

Some of the more notorious individuals who have trained at SOA include: Former Panamanian leader Manuel Noriega, now serving an extended sentence in a U.S. prison on drug charges.

El Salvador's Roberto D'Aubuisson, who formed the death squads that killed Romero and thousands of others during the Salvadoran civil war. Former Argentine President Gen. Leopoldo Galtieri, accused of making thousands of people "disappear" during Argentina's "dirty war" of the 1970s.

This whole article can be read at
http://www.cnn.com/SPECIALS/cold.war/episodes/18/spotlight/

The School of the Americas is only one shining example of what the Unknowns use to create chaos and mayhem in the countries that are rich in natural resources. Africa and South America are prime examples. They have demons all over these continents creating problems. Any well-meaning politician who goes against these scoundrels is immediately ousted. This allows their puppets to create crisis after crisis. Analogous to what they do in the United States, they scare the people into submission.

In 2006, a director of the Colombian military intelligence and a fellow officer were implicated in a series of false flag terror attacks. The attacks killed at least one person and injured 19 soldiers in the city of Bogota. These men that have been implicated, of course, are attendees or graduates of the School of the Americas. The Colombian Public Ministry investigated Colonel Horacio Arbelaez, former Director of the Army's Joint Intelligence Center, Major Javier Efren Hermida Benavides, and Captain Luis Eduardo Barrero for placing bombs in a shopping mall and other places in Bogota. This event occurred on the very eve of President Uribe's second term inauguration. As they always do, the false flag bombings were to be blamed on an enemy of the people. In this case, it was the FARC. It is no surprise that the Army Joint Intelligence Center that was directed by Colonel Horacio Arbelaez receives funding from the U.S. State Department. The same U.S. State Department responsible for funding the School of the Americas.

Source: http://www.ciponline.org/colombia/0609units01.htm

According to tapes, videos and documents, these officers reportedly were in cahoots with a FARC member who defected. Isn't that something? A terrorist leaves one terrorist group to join another. Meanwhile, Major Javier Efren Hermida Benavides, who claims to be innocent, told a Colombian radio station that the operation at the shopping mall was carried out with the full knowledge of the highest military officials. This is nothing more than what is commonly referred to as "Problem, Reaction" Solution." They create the crisis, they get the reaction of the people, and then offer the solution in order to look like our saviors. This is how they are able to suppress and oppress the people without them ever realizing who their true enemies are. This cannot be stressed enough in this book. These demons are all interconnected no matter what their race or nationality.

Despite the accusations and subsequent investigation, Colonel Horacio Arbelaez (a major suspect) became Colombia's defense ambassador in Israel. He was previously the head of intelligence for the Colombian Army's 18th Brigade based in Arauca. It is not by happenstance that Arauca is also known for being rich in oil. The Caño Limón oil fields located in its territory account for 30% of Colombian oil output. Would it surprise anyone if I said that this brigade, located in a spot that was rich in oil reserves, received extensive assistance and in-country training from U.S. Special Forces?

It is clear that graduates from the School of the Americas are put in place to uphold the policies of the criminal elite. These graduates are responsible for some of the worst human rights violations in Latin American history. It is a well accepted fact that some graduates participated in the assassination of Archbishop Oscar Romero and the El Mozote Massacre. The Salvadorian armed forces trained by the School of the Americas killed at least 1,000 civilians in an anti-guerrilla campaign. The El Mozote Massacre occurred in the village of El Mozote, in El Salvador on December 11, 1981.

ELTIEMPO.COM / ARCHIVO

Miércoles 20 de agosto de 2008

Inicio Colombia Mundo Deportes Economía Opinión Tecnología Cultura y ocio Vida de hoy Clasificados Archivo Videos Yo público Blogs

Encuentre todas las noticias de Colombia y el mundo desde 1990

Haga de eltiempo.com su página de inicio

eltiempo.com / archivo

Procuraduría implica al coronel Horacio Arbeláez Sarmiento en caso de falsos atentados

Para leer esta nota usted debe ser un usuario registrado. Regístrese o ingrese aquí.

El oficial, hoy agregado militar en Israel, era el jefe de los dos militares acusados por la Fiscalía en la seguidilla de falsos atentados ocurridos el año pasado en Bogotá.

Por el escándalo -revelado por EL TIEMPO- están llamados a juicio dos mayores de inteligencia del Ejército.

Hasta el momento, la Fiscalía solo había investigado a los mayores Javier Efr (...)

This article can be read at the following link:
http://beta.eltiempo.com/archivo/documento/CMS-3712312

Also in 2006, Colombian military officers from the Third Brigade ambushed an elite anti-drug squad in the town of Jamundí, killing ten policemen. One of the top officers in the attack, Colonel Bayron Carvajal, now under arrest, attended courses at the School of the Americas. The anti-drug squad that was attacked also trained with U.S. forces. The public is given the actual shooters (patsies) as the bad guys, while the real demons who benefited and planned the attacks are parading around as the good guys (what else is new). All of the men involved in the attack are now under arrest for collaborating with the drug cartels that they were trained to fight in the first place.

Other attendees of the School of the Americas were also involved in Operation Condor. Operation Condor archives are known as the "Archives of Terror." The dictators (military governments) of South America came together under Operation Candor to allegedly stomp out communist groups from their countries by using assassinations and other intelligence operations. This operation was supported by the CIA, whose top dog (head of the CIA) at the time just happened to be?? Drum roll pleazzze.............................big daddy Bush.

Atrocities like Operation Candor were sold as a means of combating communism. It gave the military dictatorships an excuse to kill, or imprison anyone who opposed their regime. This is now happening in Western countries under the guise of fighting terrorism.

Sources: http://www.usatoday.com/news/washington/2007-06-15-colombia_N.htm
http://www.procuraduria.gov.co/html/noticias_2006/noticias_368.htm
http://news.bbc.co.uk/1/hi/world/americas/3720724.stm

 **Associated Press**

US trained Colombian soldiers jailed for working with cartel, says human rights group

Saturday, August 18th 2007
Toby Muse, The Associated Press

BOGOTA, Colombia: Seven Colombian officers accused of working for the country's biggest cocaine cartel were trained by the U.S. military to help Colombia fight leftist rebels and its illegal drugs industry, a human rights group said Friday. The officers attended courses at the Western Hemisphere Institute for Security Cooperation — formerly called the School of the Americas — at Fort Benning in Columbus, Georgia, said School of the Americas Watch group, a leading critic of the institute.

Six are in jail on charges of conspiring with the Norte del Valle cartel, the largest and most violent cocaine-trafficking organization in Colombia, and another is on the run, the group said. School of the Americas Watch said in a statement that it matched the names of those in the scandal with its database of attendees at the institute. Calls to Colombia's Ministry of Defense were not returned and an e-mail to the school's public affairs office was not answered.

The group said Col. Byron Carvajal, who is on trial for allegedly overseeing the killings of 10 investigators and an informant of an anti-drug unit as they were carrying out a raid in 2006, received combat weapons training at the institute in 1985. Col. Alvaro Quijano who led a special counterinsurgency unit in western Colombia — a cartel stronghold — taught classes on Peacekeeping Operations and Democratic Sustainment at the school from 2003 to 2004. Quijano and other soldiers were arrested Aug. 9 and are accused of helping train the armed wing of the cartel. The soldiers are also alleged to have provided security for the Norte del Valle cartel's leader and most-wanted drug lord, Diego Montoya, who sits alongside Osama bin Laden on the FBI's 10 most-wanted list. The public prosecutor's office has said they hatched a plan to bust Montoya's brother from jail, where he is awaiting extradition to the United States on drug trafficking charges.

The School of Americas, founded in 1946, became known throughout Latin America for teaching students who went on to work in dictatorships across the region, and appearing to advocate torture and extra-judicial executions in their training manuals. It was closed in 2001 and the institute opened shortly afterward in the building, providing many of the same courses. The institute is the U.S. Defense Department's largest Spanish-language training facility for Latin America's military and law-enforcement officers.

Officers of Colombia's armed forces have long been accused of working with the country's far-right death squads, which continue to kill union members, leftist rebels and suspected collaborators. Colombia has received around US$5 billion (€3.72 billion) in aid in the past seven years, much of it for Colombia's security forces. U.S. aid to Colombia is under greater scrutiny as the Democrat-controlled Congress criticizes the military's human rights record and failure to stem the cocaine industry.

Also refer to: http://news.bbc.co.uk/2/hi/americas/7389430.stm

On September 20, 1996, the Pentagon made seven training manuals available to the public. These manuals were produced by the U.S. military for the School of the Americas and were training manuals used in most Latin American countries. Based on much older manuals that were similar to those found in what is referred to as "Project X," the training manuals go as far back as 1982. Project X was part of a U.S. Army foreign intelligence assistance program during the 1960s. Project X was known to have been a military effort to create intelligence field manuals that were directly drawn from the counterinsurgency experiences in Vietnam. The manuals taught torture interrogation and human resource exploitation training. The seven manuals contained training in motivation by fear, how to place bounties for enemy dead, false imprisonment, torture, execution, and kidnapping a target's family members.

A bill to abolish the school with 134 co-sponsors was introduced to the House Armed Services Committee in 2005. In June 2007, the McGovern/Lewis Amendment to shut off funding for the school failed by six votes. This effort to close the school was endorsed by the non-partisan Council on Hemispheric Affairs, who called the Institute a "Black eye."

Source: http://thomas.loc.gov/cgi-bin/bdquery/z?d109:h.r.01217:

Torture is Un-American: The SOA and its Devastating Legacy

Today, an attempt will be made to eliminate the final refuge of the former School of the Americas (SOA), an immensely controversial military training base for "qualified citizens of the Western Hemisphere," located in Fort Benning, Georgia and funded by U.S. taxpayers. Representative James McGovern (D-Massachusetts) will introduce an amendment to the FY 2007 Foreign Operations Appropriations Bill, proposing the elimination of funding for SOA's re-incarnate: the Western Hemispheric Institute for Security Cooperation (WHINSEC). This facility was opened on January 17, 2001, after Congress officially closed the SOA in December 2000 due to its foul aroma, and established WHINSEC in its place. SOA's divisive past includes the use of military training manuals, which instructed students in the implementation of torture as an acceptable method for obtaining information from potential suspects.

Scores of SOA's graduates eventually became Latin America's military dictators or their servitors, as well as becoming prime human rights abusers. They put their U.S. acquired military training to demoniac use in the late 1970s and early 1980s. Violations included detaining civilians indefinitely, employing torture tactics, "disappearing" victims and engaging in an entire range of unspeakable abuses, which blatantly violated fundamental human rights. Its critics therefore insisted that the SOA be closed down, but sanitized by a name change, the facilities remained open. Critics argue that such torture facilities are un-American, and are not consonant with the best aspects of U.S. military tradition.

The legitimacy of the School of the America's and its successor institution, WHINSEC, diminishes exponentially upon examining the facility's history. SOA's graduate roster is teeming with pathological alumni including infamous Panamanian dictator and convicted drug trafficker Manuel Noriega, ex-head of the Argentine military junta Leopoldo Galtierri, and organizer of Salvadoran death squads and author of the assassination of Archbishop Oscar Romero, Roberto D' Aubuisson. In the 1989 El Salvadoran massacre, 19 out of the 26 individuals, who were implicated in the killing of 6 Jesuit priests and a female employee at a Jesuit mission along with her teenage daughter, happened to be SOA graduates.

This document can be found in it's entirety at http://www.coha.org/2006/06/torture-is-un-american-the-soa-and-its-devastating-legacy/

In 2004, Venezuela became the first South American country to cease all training of Venezuelan soldiers at WHINSEC (School of Americas). The demons that work behind the scenes put their slimy paws into different countries around the world in various ways—influencing and medaling in the politics of sovereign nations. In Latin America, two of the most common are drug operations and placing their minions in high positions of the military and politics. Hence, the vast wealth that stems from the abundance of natural resources in South America is in the hands of a few.

EXPERIMENTING ON THE HUMAN CATTLE

We need to understand that the human devils who work behind the scenes consider the masses of people to be nothing more than cattle. They have been experimenting on their cattle for a very long time. Everyone is familiar with the Tuskegee experiment and Agent Orange. Please understand that those two incidents are only two drops in the bucket of what they have done to the human populace.

In the July of 2008, it was revealed that the powers that be wanted to test nerve gas on Australian solders during the Cold War. Recently declassified Australian Government documents reveal that the United States was attempting to persuade the then Prime Minister, Harold Holt, to permit tests of Sarin nerve gas on his soldiers.

CDC Home

CDC Centers for Disease Control and Prevention
Your Online Source for Credible Health Information

In 1932, the Public Health Service, working with the Tuskegee Institute, began a study to record the natural history of syphilis in hopes of justifying treatment programs for blacks. It was called the "Tuskegee Study of Untreated Syphilis in the Negro Male."

The study initially involved 600 black men – 399 with syphilis, 201 who did not have the disease. The study was conducted without the benefit of patients' informed consent. Researchers told the men they were being treated for "bad blood," a local term used to describe several ailments, including syphilis, anemia, and fatigue. In truth, they did not receive the proper treatment needed to cure their illness. In exchange for taking part in the study, the men received free medical exams, free meals, and burial insurance. Although originally projected to last 6 months, the study actually went on for 40 years.

Read the entire article at: http://www.cdc.gov/tuskegee/timeline.htm

US planned nerve gas tests on Australian soldiers

Article from: AAP

Font size: a a   Email article: Print article: Submit comment:

July 06, 2008 08:05am

THE US military planned to test deadly nerve gas on Australian soldiers in far north Queensland during the Cold War, declassified documents reveal.

The Defence and Prime Minister's office files show that the US was strongly pushing then prime minister Harold Holt's government in the 1960s to allow tests of two of the deadliest chemical weapons ever developed -- VX and GB, better known as Sarin nerve gas.

The revelation airs this morning on the Nine Network's *Sunday* program.

It says the top secret plan involved allowing 200 mainly Australian combat troops to be aerially bombed and sprayed with the chemical weapons.

It's understood the Iron Range rainforest near Lockhart River in far north Queensland was the likely location for the tests.

Peter Bailey, a former senior official with Mr Holt, tells the program the request caused consternation in Canberra, and as far as he knows the tests never went ahead.

But he says planning was very advanced in the US, which wanted the operation to be kept secret because the weapons were illegal under international law.

Declassified documents reveal the US military planned to test deadly nerve gas on Australian soldiers during the Cold War. 7/2008...

This article and video clip of Australia's Skynews channel can be viewed at:
http://www.news.com.au/couriermail/story/0,23739,23976753-952,00.html
Also refer to: *http://news.brisbanetimes.com.au/national/us-planned-to-test-nerve-gas-on-aussies-20080706-32e7.html*

In the summer of 1966, the United States Army Medical Command called Fort Detrick ran special operations tests in the New York subway system. In these tests, bacteria-filled light bulbs were dropped onto the tracks from moving trains. The bacteria released from the bulbs created the spread of Bacillus Globigii. Another dangerous bacterium called Bacillus Subtilis was also used on U.S. service people during Project Shipboard Hazard and Defense. This project is commonly known as

"SHAD" or Project 112. SHAD was a series of test conducted by the U.S. Department of Defense during the Cold War era consisting of biological weapons and chemical weapons. The tests were conducted on unwilling and uninformed military personnel. Revelations concerning the project were first exposed and brought to light by an independent producer and investigative journalist by the name of Eric Longabardi of the TeleMedia News Productions. In the world of double speak, the Department of Veteran's Affairs stated:

> **"Service members were not test subjects, but rather were involved in conducting the tests. Animals were used in some, but not most, tests. "**
> *Source*: http://www1.va.gov/shad/

In other words, they were not test subjects. They were the subjects of the test. Can someone say "Double speak?"

In 2005, the Department of Homeland Security sprayed what they referred to as a non-toxic agent into New York's Grand Central Station. The goal was to allegedly examine how chemicals might flow through the terminal in a terrorist attack. However, they never disclosed exactly which chemical was released into the station. They always do these things without the consent of the people. But then again, does a rancher or a farmer ask his herd of cattle for permission to run test and experiments? Can you see that we are basically hanging by a thread? Human beings better stop fighting about silliness and start focusing on real issues. Skin Heads, Ku Klux Klan members, and the Aryan Nation better wake up and stop thinking blacks and Latinos are their enemy. Black Nationalist and black militants better wake up and stop thinking that "Da white man did this" or "Da white man did that to us." I am sorry to burst your bubble, but "Da white man" has not done a damn thing! The white race has never had the power to do anything, nor will they ever have it.

The white race and the white supremacy doctrine have been used and were created by the Unknowns in order to create chaos. But we will save that discussion for another day. The point here is that those operating behind the scenes, guiding human events, could care less about your skin color or nationality. As I have documented here in this section, they have and are experimenting on all of us! White folk are not exempt. But do not believe me. Ask the white Australians or the white American sailors sprayed with nerve gas by their own defense department!

These men are joining the armed forces to help protect their country from bad people. Instead, they were used like lab rats by worse people than the ones they were trained to fight. Do you see why we are having so much trouble? It is because we do not know who the real enemies are. We are always looking for enemies outside, instead of looking in our own house first. Yesterday, it was the Russians and Communism. Today, it is the Arabs and terrorism.

> *If Tyranny and Oppression come to this land, it will be in the guise of fighting a foreign enemy.* – James Madison (1751-1836), 4th U.S. President

Sources:
http://www.pbs.org/wgbh/amex/weapon/timeline/timeline2.html
http://ijs.sgmjournals.org/cgi/reprint/51/1/35.pdf
http://americanrevival.org/quotes/forefathers.htm

Monday, 13 February 2006, 15:31 GMT

Hidden history of US germ testing

Fifty years ago, American scientists were in a frantic race to counter what they saw as the Soviet threat from germ warfare. Biological pathogens they developed were tested on volunteers from a pacifist church and were also released in public places.

The remarkable story is told in a BBC Radio 4 documentary, Hotel Anthrax.

(in part)..........

Subway experiment

But it wasn't just the white coat volunteers and sailors who were subject to experiments. Scientists used what they thought was a harmless simulant in major bio-weapon tests across US cities and on public transport. It was a bacteria which they believed was harmless but which would mimic the dispersal of deadly biological agents such as anthrax.

But later research showed that the strain of Bacillus globigii, or BG, did pose a risk to people who were ill or whose immune system was failing. The programme hears from a retired scientist whose job in 1966 was to drop light bulbs carrying BG on the New York subway. He would then measure how the simulant might spread in the event of a real attack, using a motorised vacuum devise concealed inside a suitcase.

Wally Pannier, 82, recalls: "We'd just drop light bulbs with the powdered stimulant inside. "I think it spread pretty good because you had a natural aerosol developed every few minutes from every train that went past."

In 1994, the Senate Committee on Veterans' Affairs conducted what it described as a comprehensive analysis stretching back 50 years of the extent to which veterans were exposed to potentially dangerous substances without knowledge or consent.

You can read this complete article at:
http://news.bbc.co.uk/1/hi/programmes/file_on_4/4701196.stm

These types of experiments are still going on today. Do not think that this cruelty is a thing of the past. Currently, there are still soldiers that are getting mysterious injections. These injections are given to them by mysterious doctors. Then, when the soldiers get sick, they get discharged. They send the soldiers home to die a painful death. If you think this cannot be true today, you are living in "la la" land. Ignoring reality or turning the other way is not going to make these demons go away.

Former Marine Claims Illness From Mystery Vaccine

Military Source Believes Experimental Shots May Have Been Given

POSTED: 3:03 pm EDT May 7, 2007
UPDATED: 6:53 pm EDT May 8, 2007

CLERMONT COUNTY, Ohio -- Target 5 has discovered that an alarming number of U.S. troops are having severe reactions to some of the vaccines they receive in preparation for going overseas.

"This is the worst cover-up in the history of the military," said an unidentified military health officer who fears for his job. A shot from a syringe is leaving some U.S. servicemen and women on the brink of death.

"When the issue, I believe, of the use of the vaccine comes out, I believe it will make the Walter Reed scandal pale in comparison," said the health officer. Lance Corporal David Fey, 20, has dialysis three days a week. His kidneys are failing, his military career is over, and he feels like his country

*abandoned him. "I can't look at my old pictures. I really can't,"
said Fey. "I start looking at my old pictures, and I start crying."*

*Fey grew up amid the farm fields of Clermont County.
"I never missed a day at school," he said. "I was never sick. I
was never sick."
A passion for sports and a sense of patriotism prompted the
Blanchester High School athlete to join the Marines the day he
turned 18. "I looked at every branch, but I wanted the Marine
Corps, because the Marine Corps was the few and the proud,"
said Fey.*

*Fey said he loved every minute of boot camp and combat
training at 29 Palms in California. But on Nov. 28, 2005, his life
would change forever. Fey was one of a group of Marines who
lined up for an undisclosed shot.*

*"They asked us our name. We stood on these yellow footprints,
and they gave us this shot, and we got the rest of the day off," he
recalled. "After that shot, I started swelling up. I gained 30
pounds of water. My eyes swelled up where I couldn't see. I
started snoring. I developed a rash on my hand." Three weeks
later, Fey was back in Clermont County on his death bed at
Clinton Memorial Hospital. His kidneys were failing, and his
body was so swollen that it left stretch marks.*

*"I would pray a lot," said Fey's mother, Cindy. "I would pray a
lot, 'God take him.' When I couldn't hug my son because he
would scream in pain or yell at me for touching him and stuff, I
used to pray to God, 'just take him tonight.'" Cindy Fey began
pouring over medical records in search of answers. She said the
shot was never listed in he son's medical records. The military
claimed he never received a shot. But as Target 5 discovered,
the military's story would change.*

*The Department of Defense stated that "all service members'
vaccinations are documented in the individual's permanent
medical record." But Fey's military medical records revealed no
shot on that day. Another Marine in Fey's unit told Target 5 that*

there is no shot listed in his medical records either and also said that the people who administered the shot never told his unit what it was.

When Cindy Fey called the U.S. Marine Hospital in 29 Palms to find out what kind of vaccine her son was given, she was told that the information was confidential. Eleven months later, her son's medical records were mysteriously changed with a handwritten notation indicating that the mystery shot was a flu vaccine.

The military official who spoke to Target 5 on the condition of anonymity said that it was not surprising that nothing appeared originally in Fey's records. "We have a lovely term for that," he said. "We call it C.Y.A. That's unfortunately an S.O.P. in the military." Fey is one of a growing number of U.S. servicemen and women who are getting sick after receiving vaccines. And the highly praised Department of Defense medical officer who spoke with Target 5 said that the number is up in the thousands. The symptoms range from joint aches and pains and arthritic symptoms to death.

The Department of Defense said that it encourages "healthcare workers and vaccine recipients to report adverse (reactions) events." But the military never reported Fey's reaction to the Centers for Disease Control and Prevention, and the FDA.

"I see the way the propaganda and information war is waged against America's sons and daughters and how patients are treated who claim to be injured from a vaccine," said the unidentified health officer. "That's troubling. That should trouble America." The officer said those who have claimed to have had adverse reactions to shots are treated like it is all in their heads. Asked whether servicemen and women are receiving experimental vaccines, the officer said, "I would hope to God not. But from what I've seen, I would have to say yes."

This article can be read in it's entirety at:
http://www.wlwt.com/news/13271378/detail.html

The article can be read in full at:
http://www.democracynow.org/2005/7/13/how_the_u_s_government_e
xposed

Who has been brought to justice for all of these criminal experiments? Absolutely no one has ever been arrested. But if you do not pay your taxes, you are going to jail. What are those taxes used for? They are used to pay for the same experiments they are using on us. In essence, we are paying for our own demise. One cannot help but think that the criminal elite get a kick, or a chuckle, out of that fact. Can you imagine the rape victim paying the rapist to do his deed? In our current reality, the rapist (IRS) has a lawful right to collect that payment from his victims (the people).

ЧҺе Ꭲеᴡ Ꭱork Ꭲіmеѕ

Sailors Sprayed With Nerve Gas In Cold War Test, Pentagon Says

By THOM SHANKER WITH WILLIAM J. BROAD
Published: May 24, 2002

The Defense Department sprayed live nerve and biological agents on ships and sailors in cold war-era experiments to test the Navy's vulnerability to toxic warfare, the Pentagon revealed today.

The Pentagon documents made public today showed that six tests were carried out in the Pacific Ocean from 1964 to 1968. In the experiments, nerve or chemical agents were sprayed on a variety of ships and their crews to gauge how quickly the poisons could be detected and how rapidly they would disperse, as well as to test the effectiveness of protective gear and decontamination procedures in use at the time. Hundreds of sailors exposed to the poisons in tests conducted in the 1960's could be eligible for health care benefits, and the Department of Veterans Affairs has already begun contacting those who participated in some of the experiments, known as Project Shipboard Hazard and Defense, or SHAD.

This whole article can be read at:
http://query.nytimes.com/gst/fullpage.html?res=9903E5DA163BF937A15756C0A9649C8B63

If they are experimenting on military service people, what do you think they are doing to you? Why is it that we cannot see, this is a serious beast we are up against? We might be playing games and wasting time. But I guarantee you that the enemy is busy night and day to make sure you continue to participate in your own enslavement and demise. So go ahead and call me crazy. Rest assure that while your lips are moving and you are calling me crazy, cancer is on the rise, AIDS is on the rise, heart attacks among young kids is on the rise, the sterilization of women is on the rise, erectile dysfunction is on the rise (maybe rise is not a good term), and a host of other diseases that are now prevalent in society. Most of these things were uncommon only ten or twenty years ago. I mean, who the heck knew what a prostate was fifteen years ago? Today, it is a household word. Brain tumors were also rare. However, since the introduction of aspartame (NutraSweet), by a company called G.D. Searle & Company, brain tumors have soared to new heights.

G.D. Searle & Company was led by the former U.S. Secretary of Defense, Donald Rumsfeld. From 1977 to 1985, Rumsfeld served as Chief Executive Officer, President, and also chairman of the Board of Directors of G.D. Searle. During Rumsfeld's tenure at the company, the FDA approved aspartame. It was first banned by a vote of 3-2 by the members of the review board. But as the world turns, a new FDA commissioner came on board by the name of Arthur Hayes Hull. He quickly added a new member to the review board and the next thing you know, aspartame was approved. The approval came despite the fact that in 1980, the FDA Board of Inquiry, which was made up of three independent scientists, made it clear that aspartame might induce brain tumors. The very next year, after a so-called extensive review by the FDA's own scientists, aspartame was approved as a food additive. Today it is a substitute for sugar in sugarless gum and diet soft drinks. In essence, you are trading extra calories for a possible brain tumor.

Sources: *http://www.fda.gov/bbs/topics/ANSWERS/ANS00772.html*
http://www.ehponline.org/members/2005/8711/8711.pdf

EUGENICS

Today, the most notable eugenics programs in history are those of Nazi Germany. However, the truth of the matter is that the Nazis based their eugenics program on the American programs of forced sterilization. Although early on most of the programs were coming out of California, the Harriman family, with their money and influence, attempted to weed out European immigrants that were deemed to be of a lesser class. Certain groups such as Italians, Sephardic Jews, and Eastern Europeans were subject to forced sterilization. Contrary to popular belief, racism was not exclusive between blacks and whites during the turn of the twentieth century. There were many signs posted in businesses and restaurants that read, "We do not serve Italians" or "We do not serve Irish." But, who was involved in the sterilizations? The Carnegies, the Rockefellers, the Harrimans (which records show were great supporters of Hitler), other prominent families, and large corporations. The Rockefeller Foundation, which was founded by John D. Rockefeller, his son John D. Rockefeller Jr., and their principal business and philanthropic advisor Frederick T. Gates, were major players in American eugenics. They basically introduced birth control and were also the major financial contributors to women's contraception. This contribution to birth control has different parts. One part was to slow down the birth rate. These are the same people who have orchestrated the women's rights movement.

They do not care about women's rights or anyone else's rights. One of their goals was to get the woman out of the house in order to break-up the family structure. The whole feminist movement is maintained and controlled by the Unknowns. The Hollywood director (Fiddler on the Roof, Trading Places) and documentary film maker Aaron Russo has publicly stated that Nick Rockefeller personally told him about the criminal elite's plans of creating a microchipped population. Rockefeller also told Russo of how his family's foundation (the Rockefeller Foundation) had created and bankrolled the women's liberation movement. The goal, he said, was to get the woman out of the house and into the workforce. This was to have a duel affect. The first was to destroy the family structure in the United States. The other was to generate more revenue by taxing their new workforce (the working woman).

San Francisco Chronicle

Eugenics and the Nazis -- the California connection

Edwin Black
Sunday, November 9, 2003

Hitler and his henchmen victimized an entire continent and exterminated millions in his quest for a so-called Master Race. But the concept of a white, blond-haired, blue-eyed master Nordic race didn't originate with Hitler. The idea was created in the United States, and cultivated in California, decades before Hitler came to power. California eugenicists played an important, although little-known, role in the American eugenics movement's campaign for ethnic cleansing.

Eugenics was the pseudoscience aimed at "improving" the human race. In its extreme, racist form, this meant wiping away all human beings deemed "unfit," preserving only those who conformed to a Nordic stereotype. Elements of the philosophy were enshrined as national policy by forced sterilization and segregation laws, as well as marriage restrictions, enacted in 27 states. In 1909, California became the third state to adopt such laws. Ultimately, eugenics practitioners coercively sterilized some 60,000 Americans, barred the marriage of thousands, forcibly segregated thousands in "colonies," and persecuted untold numbers in ways we are just learning. Before World War II, nearly half of coercive sterilizations were done in California, and even after the war, the state accounted for a third of all such surgeries.

California was considered an epicenter of the American eugenics movement. During the 20th century's first decades, California's eugenicists included potent but little-known race scientists, such as Army venereal disease specialist Dr. Paul Popenoe, citrus magnate Paul Gosney, Sacramento banker Charles Goethe, as well as members of the California state Board of Charities and Corrections and the University of California Board of Regents. Eugenics would have been so much bizarre parlor talk had it not been for extensive financing by corporate philanthropies, specifically the Carnegie Institution, the Rockefeller Foundation and the Harriman railroad fortune. They were all in league with some of America's most respected scientists from such prestigious universities as Stanford, Yale, Harvard and Princeton. These academicians espoused race theory and race science, and then faked and twisted data to serve eugenics' racist aims.

Stanford President David Starr Jordan originated the notion of "race and blood" in his 1902 racial epistle "Blood of a Nation," in which the university scholar declared that human qualities and conditions such as talent and poverty were passed through the blood. In 1904, the Carnegie Institution established a laboratory complex at Cold Spring Harbor on Long Island that stockpiled millions of index cards on ordinary Americans, as researchers carefully plotted the removal of families, bloodlines and whole peoples. From Cold Spring Harbor, eugenics advocates agitated in the legislatures of America, as well as the nation's social service agencies and associations. <u>The Harriman railroad fortune paid local charities, such as the New York Bureau of Industries and Immigration, to seek out Jewish, Italian and other</u>

immigrants in New York and other crowded cities and subject them to deportation, confinement or forced sterilization. The Rockefeller Foundation helped found the German eugenics program and even funded the program that Josef Mengele worked in before he went to Auschwitz.

Much of the spiritual guidance and political agitation for the American eugenics movement came from California's quasi-autonomous eugenic societies, such as Pasadena's Human Betterment Foundation and the California branch of the American Eugenics Society, which coordinated much of their activity with the Eugenics Research Society in Long Island. These organizations -- which functioned as part of a closely-knit network -- published racist eugenic newsletters and pseudoscientific journals, such as Eugenical News and Eugenics, and propagandized for the Nazis.

This article can be read in full at: *http://www.sfgate.com/cgi-bin/article.cgi?file=/chronicle/archive/2003/11/09/ING9C2QSKB1.DTL*
Also refer to:
http://www.nature.com/embor/journal/v5/n5/full/7400158.html

These demons are now forcing our children to get more vaccinations at birth and more vaccinations before registering for school. The government is basically now telling us what medicine to put in our bodies. Perhaps only conspiracy theorist like me find that troubling.

> **"If people let government decide what foods they eat and what medicines they take, their bodies will soon be in as sorry a state as are the souls of those who live under tyranny."**

– Thomas Jefferson

OUTRO

Take this written documentary and use it like a bucket of water to wake up the sleepful ones. Take this written documentary and use it as a weapon against all enemies—foreign and domestic. Take this written documentary and use it as a text book that can teach the downtrodden, the hapless, the helpless, the tyrannized, and the oppressed. Teach them how to get up out of the muck and mire. Take this written documentary and use it to change those who believe, into those who know. Remember, with knowledge there is power and freedom; but with ignorance, there is mental slavery.

"THE FIRST TEMPERATURE"

GLOSSARY OF WORDS & TERMS

Abhor- To fill or be filled with horror or disgust.

Abnormal- Not normal, average, typical, or usual; deviates from a standard.

18th Parallel- The 18th parallel north is a circle of latitude that is 18 degrees north of the Earth's equatorial plane.

Academics- Acquired by formal education, esp. at a college or university.

Acquiesce- To assent tacitly; submit or comply silently or without protest; agree; consent.

Akin- Essentially similar, related, or compatible.

American Enterprise Institute- Is a conservative think tank, founded in 1943. According to the institute its mission is "to defend the principles and improve the institutions of American freedom and democratic capitalism — limited government, private enterprise, individual liberty and responsibility, vigilant and effective defense and foreign policies, political accountability, and open debate. However, this is just a smoke screen. AEI has emerged as one of the leading architects of the second Bush administration's public policy. More than twenty AEI alumni and current visiting scholars and fellows have served either in a Bush administration policy post or on one of the governments many panels and commissions.

American Eugenics Society- Was a society established in 1922 to promote eugenics in the United States. It was the result of the Second International Conference on Eugenics (New York, 1921, same year that the CFR was established). The founders included Madison Grant, Harry H. Laughlin, Irving Fisher, Henry Fairfield Osborn, and Henry Crampton. The organization started by promoting racial betterment, eugenic health, and genetic education through public lectures, exhibits at county fairs ea., but under the direction of Frederick Osborn, started to place greater focus on issues of population control, genetics, and, later, medical genetics. In 1972 the AES was reorganized and renamed in "*The Society for the Study of Social Biology*".

Amero- The Amero is the theoretical name of the North American currency union. It was first proposed in 1999 by Canadian economist Herbert G. Grubel. A senior fellow of the conservative Fraser Institute think-tank, he published a book entitled *The Case for the Amero* in September 1999, the year that the euro became a virtual currency. Another Canadian think-tank, the C.D. Howe Institute, advocates the creation of a shared currency between Canada, Mexico and the United States.

Ammonium nitrate- Is a Chemical Compound with the chemical formula NH_4NO_3, and it is a white powder at room temperature and standard pressure. It is commonly used in agriculture as a high-nitrogen fertilizer, and it has also been used as an oxidizing agent in explosives, including improvised explosive devices.

Apartheid- An official policy of racial segregation formerly practiced in the Republic of South Africa, involving political, legal, and economic discrimination against nonwhites.

Army Fatigues- Military clothes or apparel that meshes with a particular environment.

Articulated- Made clear or distinct.

Astray- Away from that which is right; into error, confusion, or undesirable action or thought

Astronomical- Enormously or inconceivably large or great.

Augusto Pinochet- (November 25, 1915 - December 10, 2006) was a Chilean military officer and dictator. He was the leader of the Government Junta of Chile from 1973 to 1974 and President of Chile from 1974 until the return of democratic rule in 1990.

Bacillus Globigii- A species of bacillus found in soil and decomposing organic matter; some strains produce antibiotics.

Biological Weapons Convention- Was the first multilateral disarmament treaty banning the production of an entire category of weapons. It was the result of prolonged efforts by the international community to establish a new instrument that would supplement the 1925 Geneva Protocol.

Bioluminescence- Is the production and emission of light by a living organism as the result of a chemical reaction during which chemical energy is converted to light energy. Its name is a hybrid word, originating from the Greek *bios* for "living" and the Latin *lumen* "light".

Blacklist- A list of persons under suspicion, disfavor, censure, etc.

Blue Blood- Originally from the Spanish Term *Sangre Azul*. Not only a member of wealthy family, but a member of an established one.

Campus Watch- Is an organization which "reviews and critiques Middle East studies in North America with an alleged aim to improving them." It is a project of the Middle East Forum, an American, neoconservative, pro-Israel think tank. It is based in Philadelphia, Pennsylvania, U.S. and was founded in 2002 by Daniel Pipes. It is currently headed by Winfield Myers.

Carte Blanche- French word meaning blank check, or blank document. It is used to refers to full discretionary power.

Cahoots- Usually used to refer to persons who are in a Partnership or league. Originates from the French *cahute* meaning cabin, hut. The term came to mean, "those who are in the same cabin or hut".

Circa- Literally means "about" or "around". It is widely used when the dates of historical events are *approximately* known.

Clandestine- Done or kept in secret, sometimes to conceal an illicit or improper purpose.

Compartmentalized- Divided into compartments or assignments so that each compartment (person) does not know the full picture or intention of an organization or group. To separate something into different categories or compartments.

Confined- To keep within limits.

Conjure up- To make up or bring about from scratch. To bring forth a claim with no basis in fact.

Consolidation- The process of uniting : the quality or state of being united; *specifically* the unification of two or more corporations by dissolution of existing ones and creation of a single new corporation.

Consular officer- A Consular is an official representative of the government of one country or state in the territory of another, normally acting to assist and protect the citizens of the consulars own country. A person of or pertaining to a *consul*, or the office thereof.

Conundrum- An intricate and difficult problem. *Also*; a question or problem having only a conjectural answer.

Counterinsurgency- Organized military activity designed to combat insurgency.

Coup d'etat- A sudden and decisive action in politics, esp. one resulting in a change of government illegally or by force.

Culprit- The source or cause of a problem.

Demonize- To be made to look evil or to be made to look like an enemy of another.

Dialogue- A conversation between two or more persons to attain knowledge or an understanding of a topic.

Deities- The word "deity" derives from the Latin *"dea"*, ("goddess"), and *'"deus"*, ("god"). Related are words for "sky": the Latin *"dies"* ("day") and *"divum"* ("open sky"), and the Sanskrit *"div,"* *"diu"* ("sky," "day," "shine"). Also related are "divine" and "divinity," from the Latin *"divinus,"* from *"divus."*

Discredit- To cause disbelief in the accuracy or authority of a report or claim or to deprive of good repute.

Distinguish- To perceive a difference in. Also, to single out or take special notice of.

Doctrine- A particular principle, position, or policy taught or advocated, as of a religion or government.

Document- An original or official paper relied on as the basis, proof, or support of something.

Dossiers- Files containing detailed records on a particular person or subject.

Double Speak- Language used to deceive usually through concealment or misrepresentation of truth. It is meant to disguise or distort the actual intention of the person(s) doing the double speaking.

Due Diligence- Research and analysis of a topic or subject. Background check on a person or corporation/company done in preparation for a business transaction.

Enzymes- Are biomolecules that catalyze (*i.e.* increase the rates of) chemical reactions. Nearly all enzymes are proteins.

Epoch- A defining moment in the beginning of, or characteristic of, a distinctive historical period or era.

Escalation Rhetoric- Rhetoric or comments intended to escalate or create an event.

Etymology- Is the study of the history of words establishing when they entered a language, from what source, and how their form and meaning have changed over time.

Eugenics- The science of improving stock, whether human or animal. Also, A social philosophy which advocates the improvement of human hereditary qualities through selective breeding or experimentation.

False Flag Operation- Are covert operations conducted by governments, corporations, or other organizations, which are designed to appear as though they are being carried out by other entities. The name is derived from the military concept of flying false colors; that is, flying the flag of a country other than one's own. False flag operations are not limited to war and counter-insurgency operations, and have been used in peace-time.

Federal registry- Is the official daily publication for rules, proposed rules, and notices of Federal agencies and organizations, as well as executive orders and other presidential documents.

Filibuster- Is a form of obstruction in a legislature or other decision-making body. An attempt is made to infinitely extend debate upon a proposal in order to delay the progress or completely prevent a vote on the proposal taking place. The term 'filibuster' was first used in 1851. It was derived from the Spanish *filibustero* meaning 'pirate' or 'freebooter'. This term had in turn evolved from the French word *flibustier*, which itself evolved from the Dutch *vrijbuiter* (freebooter). This term was applied at the time to American adventurers, mostly from Southern states, who sought to overthrow the governments of

Central American states, and was transferred to the users of the filibuster, seen as a tactic for pirating or hijacking debate.

First Zionist congress- Is the name given to the congress held in Basel (Basle), Switzerland, from August 29 to August 31, 1897. It was the first congress of the Zionist Organization (ZO) (to become the World Zionist Organization (WZO) in 1960). It was called for and chaired by Theodor Herzl, the founder of modern Zionism. The major achievements of the Congress were its formulation of the Zionist platform, known as the Basle program, the foundation of the World Zionist Organization, and the adoption of Hatikvah as its anthem (already the anthem of Hovevei Zion and later to become the national anthem of the State of Israel).

Futile- Serving no useful purpose : completely ineffective.

Generic- Having no particularly distinctive quality or application. Being or having a nonproprietary name

Globalization- To extend to other or all parts of the globe; make worldwide.

Grand Lodge- Is the usual governing body of "Craft", or "Blue Lodge", Freemasonry in a particular jurisdiction. The first Masonic Grand Lodge was established in England in 1717 as the Premier Grand Lodge of England.

Hashem- Literally means "the name" in the Hebrew language. The scribes of sacred texts took pause before copying them, and used terms of reverence so as to keep the true name of God concealed. Other Jewish Historians say that the Jews lost the right to call upon the Jehovah by name hence "Hashem" serves as a stand in name.

Hexagram- Is a six-pointed geometric star figure, the compound of two equilateral triangles. The intersection is a regular hexagon. While generally recognized as a symbol of Jewish identity it is used also in other historical, religious and cultural contexts, for example in Islam, and Eastern Religions as well as in Occultism. In mathematics, the G_2 root system is in the form of a hexagram.

Hieroglyph- A character of any logographic or partly logographic writing system. When people think of Hieroglyphics, they normally think of ancient Egyptian writing systems.

Hubris- Exaggerated pride or self-confidence.

Human Beast- The wicked who have no conscience when committing animalistic acts.

Ideology- Is an organized collection of ideas. An ideology can be thought of as a comprehensive vision, as a way of looking at things, as in common sense and several philosophical tendencies or a set of ideas proposed by the dominant class of a society to all members of this society. The main purpose behind an ideology is to offer change in society through a normative thought process. Ideologies are systems of abstract thought (as opposed to mere ideation) applied to public matters and thus make this concept central to politics. Implicitly every political tendency entails an ideology whether or not it is propounded as an explicit system of thought.

Idiom An expression whose meaning is not predictable from the usual meanings of its constituent elements, as *kick the bucket* or *hang one's head,* or from the general grammatical rules of a language, as *the table round* for *the round table,* and that is not a constituent of a larger expression of like characteristics.

IEEE- Is an acronym for Institute of Electrical and Electronics Engineers.

Ill-informed- Not being informed. Either intentionally by someone else or by ones own ignorance of a subject.

Implemented- To carry out a doctrine or scheme for a specific purpose.

Inconsistencies- Not being consistent or a string of consistency broken by an inconsistent event or subject.

Infiltration- To enter or become established in the opposition gradually or unobtrusively usually for subversive purposes.

Information- The communication or reception of knowledge or intelligence. Also, knowledge obtained from investigation, study, or instruction.

Infra- Used to refer to something that will be discussed later.

Inimical- Reflecting or indicating hostility or having the disposition of an enemy.

Innocuous- Not noticeable; not likely to give offense or to arouse strong feelings or hostility.

Instantaneously- Occurring or present at a particular time without any delay being purposely introduced.

Intrigues- To arouse the interest, desire, or curiosity of.

Jean-Paul Sartre- Was born Jean-Paul Charles Aymard Sartre (June 21, 1905 – April 15, 1980), but is normally known simply as Jean-Paul Sartre, was a French existentialist philosopher and pioneer, dramatist and screenwriter, novelist and critic. He was a leading figure in 20th century French philosophy.

Knowledge- Is (i) expertise, and skills acquired by a person through experience or education; the theoretical or practical understanding of a subject, (ii) what is known in a particular field or in total; facts and information or (iii) awareness or familiarity gained by experience of a fact or situation. Philosophical debates in general start with Plato's formulation of knowledge as "justified true belief". There is however no single agreed definition of knowledge presently, nor any prospect of one, and there remain numerous competing theories. Knowledge acquisition involves complex cognitive processes: perception, learning, communication, association and reasoning. The term *knowledge* is also used to mean the confident understanding of a subject with the ability to use it for a specific purpose if appropriate.

Laissez-faire- Is a French phrase literally meaning "Let do." It stipulates that government should not interference with trade.

Lobby A group of persons who work or conduct a campaign to influence members of a legislature to vote according to the group's special interest.

Magnum Opus- The greatest achievement of an artist or writer.

Masoretic- The Masoretic Text (**MT**) is the Hebrew text of the Jewish Bible (Tanakh). It defines not just the books of the Jewish canon, but also the precise letter-text of the biblical books in Judaism, as well as their vocalization and accentuation for both public reading and private study. The MT is also widely used as the basis for translations of the Old Testament in Protestant Bibles, and in recent decades also for Catholic Bibles. The MT was primarily copied, edited and distributed by a group of Jews known as the Masoretes between the seventh and tenth centuries CE.

Mao Zedong - (26 December 1893 – 9 September 1976) was a Chinese military and political leader who led the Communist Party of China (CPC) to victory against the Kuomintang (KMT) in the Chinese Civil War, and was the leader of the People's Republic of China (PRC) from its establishment in 1949 until his death in 1976. He is part of a long list of communist that was assisted in his assent to power by the U.S. and Britain.

Mayer Rothschild- (February 23, 1744 – September 19, 1812) was the founder of the Rothschild family banking empire that would become one of the most successful business families in history. In 2005, he was ranked 7th on the Forbes magazine list of the *The Twenty Most Influential Businessmen Of All Time.* The business magazine referred to him as a "founding father of international finance".

Mendacious- Given to or characterized by deception or falsehood or divergence from absolute truth. Basically lying.

Merits- Character or conduct deserving reward, honor, or esteem.

Methods- A systematic procedure, technique, or mode of inquiry employed by or proper to a particular discipline or art.

Microcosm- A smaller system, idea or event which is representative of or analogous to a larger one.

Mind Boggling- Intellectually or emotionally overwhelming.

Modus operandi- Is often used in the abbreviated forms M.O. or simply "Method" is actually a Latin phrase, approximately translated as "mode of operation.

Mossad- The Mossad (HaMossad leModi'in v'leTafkidim Meyuhadim) (Hebrew:המוסד למודיעין ולתפקידים מיוחדים - Institute for Intelligence and Special Operations) is the national Intelligence agency of Israel. "Mossad" is the Hebrew word for institute or institution.

Mujahedeen- (Arabic مجاهد, *muğāhid*, literally "struggler") is a Muslim involved in a *jihad*, *id est* fighting in a war or involved in any other struggle. The plural is Mujahideen (Arabic: مجاهدين, *muğāhidīn*). The word is from the same Arabic triliteral as *jihad* ("struggle"). In Islamic scripture, the *mujahid* contrasts with the *qaid*, one who does not join the jihad.

Mushroom Cloud- A cloud of smoke and debris shaped like a mushroom, especially one created by the detonation of a nuclear bomb.

Neoconservative- An intellectual and political movement in favor of political, economic, and social conservatism that arose in opposition to the perceived liberalism of the 1960s.

Nil- Nothing; zero.

Nocturnal- Of, relating to, or occurring in the night. Nocturnal animals generally have highly developed senses of hearing and smell, and specially adapted eyesight.

Obliterating- To do away with completely so as to leave no trace.

Obstruction- One that stops, prevents or gets in the way of an obstacle, person or investigation.

Orwellian- Of, relating to, or evocative of the works of George Orwell, especially the satirical novel *1984,* which depicts a futuristic totalitarian state.

OSS- The Office of Strategic Services (**OSS**) was a United States intelligence agency formed during World War II. It was the wartime intelligence agency and was the predecessor to the Central Intelligence Agency.

Ostensible- Being such in appearance: plausible rather than demonstrably true or real.

Partaking- To take or have a part or share; participate.

Paul Warburg- (August 10, 1868 — January 24, 1932) was a German-American banker and early advocate of the U.S Federal Reserve system. Warburg was born into a successful Jewish banking family in Hamburg, Germany. He and his brothers Max Warburg and Felix Warburg were partners in the family firm of M.M.Warburg & CO, but while Max remained in Germany as head of that business, Felix and Paul moved to New York City in 1901, where they purchased partnerships in the investment firm of Kuhn, Loeb & Co., where at the time, the influential Jacob Schiff, his wife's brother-in-law, was senior partner. Paul Warburg became known as a persuasive advocate of central banking in America, in 1907 publishing *"Defects and Needs of Our Banking System"* in the New York Times and *"A Plan for A Modified Central Bank"*. His efforts were successful in 1913 with the founding of the United States' Federal Reserve, to which he was appointed a member of the first Federal Reserve Board by President Woodrow Wilson. In 1919 he founded and became first chairman of the American Acceptance Council. He became a director of the Council on Foreign Relations at its founding in 1921, remaining on the board until 1932.

Paul Wolfowits- (Born December 22, 1943) is a former United States Ambassador to Indonesia, U.S. Deputy Secretary of Defense, and former President of the World Bank.

Phallus- A representation of an erect penis symbolizing fertility or potency.

Phontinus pyrallis- A type of lightning bug found in North America. This firefly is harvested by the biochemical industry for the organic compounds luciferin (which is the chemical the firefly uses for its bioluminescence).

Preemtive (war)- Is waged in an attempt to repel or defeat a perceived inevitable offensive or invasion, or to gain a strategic advantage in an impending (allegedly unavoidable) war. *Preemptive war* is often confused with the term preventive war. While the latter is generally considered to violate international law, and to fall short of the requirements of a just war, *preemptive wars* are more often argued to be justified or justifiable.

Preamble- An introductory statement ; especially : the introductory part of a constitution or statute that usually states the reasons for and intent of the law.

Proffered- To offer for acceptance; tender. The act of proffering; an offer. In law, to offer, give or enter evidence.

Prominent- Widely and popularly known.

Propaganda- The spreading of ideas, information, or rumor for the purpose of helping or injuring an institution, a cause, or a person.

Provocateurs- One employed to associate with suspected persons and by pretending sympathy with their aims to incite them to some incriminating action.

Ransacked- To search carefully for plunder; to pillage.

Recess appointment- Occurs when the President of the United States fills a vacant federal position during a recess of the United States Senate. The appointment must be approved by the Senate by the end of the next session, or the position becomes vacant again. Recess appointments are authorized by Article II, Section 2 of the U.S. Constitution: "The President shall have Power to fill up all Vacancies that may happen during the Recess of the Senate, by granting Commissions which shall expire at the End of their next Session."

Reichstag- Is the seat of the German Parliament, and one of Berlin's most historical landmarks.

Relevant facts- Having significant and demonstrable bearing on the facts or truth at hand.

Remotely- Acting, acted on, or controlled indirectly or from a distance.

Responsibility- The quality or state of being responsible. The ability to respond or give a response.

Revamp- To remake or change over or revise.

Rhodes scholars- A holder of one of numerous scholarships founded under the will of Cecil J. Rhodes that can be used at Oxford University for two or three years and are open to candidates from the Commonwealth of Nations and the United States.

Rubber stamping- Authorizing or stamping legal documents without examining its merits.

Scholarly work- Also can be referred to as the "Scholarly method" is the body of principles and practices used by scholars to make their claims about the world as valid and trustworthy as possible, and to make them known to the scholarly public.

Secede- To withdraw from an organization or group. To step down from authority or a high rank.

Seneschals- An agent or steward in charge of a lord's estate in feudal times. An officer of the Kings Court.

Septuagint- Is the Koine Greek version of the Hebrew Bible, translated in stages between the 3rd and 1st centuries BC in Alexandria.

Shaw Statutes- William Schaw, on 28 December 1598, in his capacity as Master of Works and General Warden of the master masons, issued "The Statutes and ordinances to be observed by all the master masons. Schaw's first statutes root themselves in the Old Charges, with additional material to describe a hierarchy of wardens, deacons and masters. This structure would ensure that masons did not take on work which they were not competent to complete, and ensured a lodge warden would be elected by the master masons, through whom the general warden could keep in touch with each particular lodge.

Sidereal Month- Is the time the Moon takes to complete one full revolution around the Earth with respect to the background stars.

Smoking gun- A reference to an object or fact that serves as conclusive evidence of a crime or similar act.

Solidify- To make secure, substantial, or firmly fixed.

Sovereignty- Is the exclusive right to control a government, a country, a people, or oneself. A sovereign is the supreme lawmaking authority.

Spew- To send or cast forth with vigor.

Straw Man Theory- Is an opponent's argument purposely based on an informal fallacy with the misrepresentation of the opponent's position. To "set up a straw man," one describes a position that superficially resembles an opponent's actual view, yet is easier to refute, then attributes that position to the opponent. For example, someone might deliberately overstate the opponent's position. While a straw man argument may work as a rhetorical technique and succeed in persuading people it carries little or no real evidential weight, since the opponent's actual argument has not been refuted.

Supra- Referring to the subject above. Used to indicate that the current citation is from the same source as the previous one.

Synodic Months- This is the average period of the Moon's orbit with respect to the sun. The synodic month is responsible for the moon's phases because the Moon's appearance depends on the position of the Moon with respect to the Sun as seen from the Earth. While the moon is orbiting the earth, the Earth is progressing in its orbit around the Sun. This means that after completing a sidereal month the Moon must move a little farther to reach the new position of the Earth with respect to the Sun. This longer period is called the *synodic* month from the Greek *syn hodô* (σὺν ὁδῷ), meaning "with the way [of the sun]".

The Trilateral Commission- A private organization, established to foster closer cooperation between America, Europe and Japan. It was founded in July 1973, at the initiative of David

Rockefeller who was Chairman of the Council on Foreign Relations at that time. The Trilateral Commission is widely seen as a counterpart to the Council on Foreign Relations. He pushed the idea of including Japan at the Bilderberg meetings he was attending but was rebuffed. Along with Zbigniew Brzezinski and a few other people, including individuals from the Brookings Institution, Council on Foreign Relations and the Ford Foundation, he convened initial meetings out of which grew the *Trilateral* organization. Other founding members included Alan Greenspan and Paul Volcker, both eventually heads of the Federal Reserve system.

Theocracy- Government under the control of a Church or state-sponsored religion.

Truth seekers- People who want to know the truth about major events and organizations that determine the way of the world.

Tulsa World newspaper- Is a daily newspaper in Tulsa, Oklahoma, USA covering general news.

Unfounded- Lacking a sound basis. Having no facts to support a theory or idea.

United States Army Corps of Engineers (USACE)- Is a federal agency and a major Army command made up of some 34,600 civilian and 650 military personnel, making it the world's largest public engineering, design and construction management agency. Although generally associated with dams, canals and flood protection in the United States, USACE is involved in a wide range of public works support to the nation and to Department of Defense throughout the world.

Unprovoked war- A war that is started by a country without being provoked by the country that is attacked.

Uranium- Is a silver-gray metallic chemical element in the actinide series of the periodic table that has the symbol **U** and atomic number 92. It has 92 protons and electrons, 6 of them valence electrons. It can have between 141 and 146 neutrons, with 146 (U-238) and 143 in its most common isotopes. Uranium has the highest atomic weight of the naturally occurring elements. Uranium is approximately 70% more dense than lead and is weakly radioactive. It occurs naturally in low concentrations (a few parts per million) in soil, rock and water, and is commercially extracted from uranium-bearing minerals such as uraninite.

US State Department- Is the Cabinet-level foreign affairs agency of the United States government, similar to foreign ministries, foreign offices, ministries of external relations, etc. in other countries. It is administered by the Secretary of State.

Verifiable- Being able to be verified or known as fact.

Zionist- Is an international political movement that originally supported the reestablishment of a homeland for the Jewish People in Palestine (Hebrew: Eretz Yisra'el, "the Land of Israel"), and continues primarily as support for the modern state of Israel.

Bibliography

-Websters New Collegiate Dictionary (8th ed. 1976), G. & C. Merriam Co.

- Mintz , Frank P. The Liberty Lobby and the American Right. Race, Conspiracy and Culture; Greenwood Press (March 27, 1985).

- Mearsheimer, John J. and Walt, Stephen M. The Israel Lobby and U.S. Foreign Policy., Farrar, Straus and Giroux - Aug 27, 2007.

- Isikoff, Michael and Corn, David Hubris: The Inside story of spin, Scandal and Selling of the Iraq war. Three rivers press, May 29, 2007.

- Garner, Bryan A. Black's Law Dictionary, Eighth Edition Boston: West Publishing Company, January 2004.

- Quigley, Carroll Tragedy & Hope, Hollywood, Calif.:Angriff Press, 1966.

-Scheb, John M. An Introduction to the American Legal System, Albany, NY :Thomas Delmar Learning, September 2001.

- Schmidt, Helmut Men and Powers: A Political Retrospective - Random House (February 10, 1990).

- Axelrod, Alan The International Encyclopedia of Secret Societies & Fraternal Orders New York: Checkmark Books, July 1998

- Barrett, David V. Secret Societies: From the Ancient and Arcane to the Modern and Clandestine London: Blandford, 1999

- Cornwell, John Hitler's Pope: The Secret History of Pius XII New York: Penguin group 1999.

- Robison, John Proofs of a Conspiracy Against All the Religions and Governments of Europe Carried on in the Secret Kessinger Publishing: August 2003

- Gwinn, Robert P., Norton, Peter B. and McHenry, Robert The New Encyclopaedia Britannica in 32 Volumes (15th Edition) Chicago: Encyclopaedia Britannica 1993.

-Columbia encyclopedia sixth edition NEW YORK: COLUMBIA UNIVERSITY PRESS, 2001–07, NEW YORK: BARTLEBY.COM, 2001–07 UPDATED: DECEMBER, 2007.

- Brzezinski, Zbigniew The Grand Chessboard: American Primacy and Its Geostrategic Imperatives New York: Basic Books, 1998.
- Stockwell, John In Search of Enemies: A CIA Story W. W. Norton & Company: March 1984.

- Casey, William Secret War Against Hitler: Washington, DC: Regnery Gateway, 1988

- BROWN, Constantine The Coming of the Whirlwind, , Chicago: Henry Regnery Company, 1964.

-The 9/11 Commission Report: Final Report of the National Commission on Terrorist Attacks Upon the United States (Authorized Edition) (Paperback) W. W. Norton & Company, (July 22, 2004).

- Woodward, Bob Plan of Attack Simon and Schuster, 2004.

- Kinzer, Stephen All the Shah's Men: An American Coup and the Roots of Middle East Terror John Wiley & Sons, August 2004

- Keating, Martin The Final Jihad: When the "Best of the Worst" Finally Come for Us Logical Figments Books, (June 1, 1996).

- Cooley, John Unholy Wars: Afghanistan, America and International Terrorism
United Press: Pluto Press, July 2002

- Dunbar, David, Brad, Reagan and Popular Mechanics, The Editors of Debunking 9/11 Myths: Why Conspiracy Theories Can't Stand Up to the Facts Hearst Communications, August 2006

- Kean, Thomas H. and Hamilton, Lee H. Without Precedent: The Inside Story of the 9/11 Commission (Vintage) USA: Vintage Books, April 2007

- Burke, Jason Al-qaeda: Casting a Shadow of Terror London: I.B. Tauris & Co., 2003

- Sahar Huneidi, Walid Khalidi A Broken Trust: Herbert Samuel, Zionism and the Palestinians 1920-1925 I.B.Tauris
-Pool, James Who Financed Hitler Simon & Schuster Adult Publishing Group, 1997

-Sutton, Anthony Wall Street and the Rise of Hitler Buccaneer Books, Inc., 2007

-Black, Edwin Nazi Nexus: America's Corporate Connections to Hitler's Holocaust Dialog Press, 2008

INDEX

C

D

E

F

G

H

I

R

S

U

T

V

W

X

Y

Z

THE SYMBOL OF THE
SACRED MOVEMENT

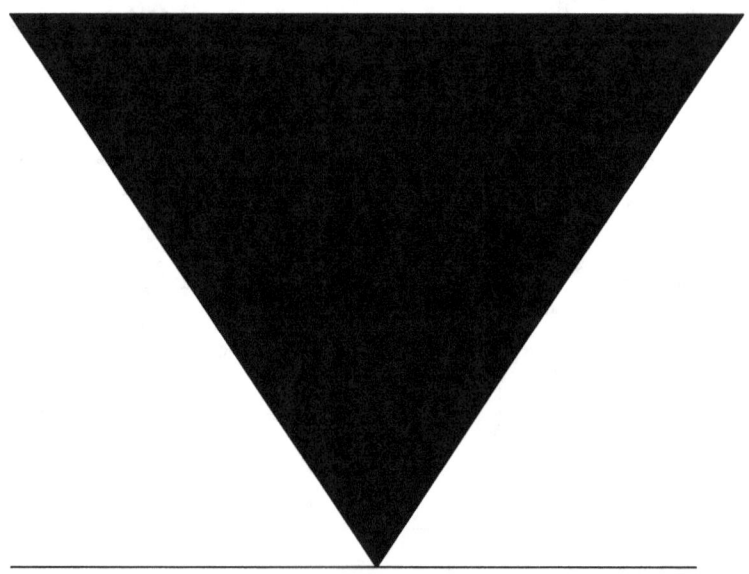